M000117250

FOREVER
YOUNG

FOREVER YOUNG

LIVING & DYING FOR CHRIST

Bridge-Logos

Gainesville, Florida 32614 USA

Forever Young

International Standard Book Number: 0-882790-9364

Library of Congress Catalog Number: Pending

Bridge-Logos Publishers

Gainesville, FL 32614

bridgelogos.com

Table of Contents

Dedication

This book is dedicated to all the young martyrs for Jesus Christ, who lived their lives and gave their lives for Him. The Church of Jesus Christ is stronger and more glorious because of those who lived and suffered and those who suffered and died.

This book is also dedicated with thanks to all the employees and volunteers of *The Voice of the Martyrs* ministry in Bartlesville, Oklahoma. For their heartfelt devotion and dedication to the persecuted Church is absolutely inspiring. Perhaps the most inspiring thing of all was seeing and hearing how much they were blessed by being able to help persecuted Christians. Tears of compassion and joy flow easily there.

Contacting the Voice of the Martyrs

The Voice of the Martyrs can be contacted as follows:

P.O. Box 443

Bartlesville, OK, 74005

918-337-8015

thevoice@vom-usa.org

Visit their website for young people at:
http://www.linkingup.com

What Is a Christian Martyr?

The word "martyr" is from the Greek word for "witness." All of my dictionaries agree that a martyr is one or all of three things:

1. One who chooses to suffer death rather than renounce religious principles.

2. One who makes great sacrifices or suffers much in order to further a belief, cause, or principle.

3. One who endures great suffering.

If we combine these definitions, we understand a Christian martyr to be:

1. A person who witnesses for Jesus Christ by choosing to suffer death rather than renounce Him or His works.

2. A person who makes great sacrifices or suffers much as a witness for Jesus Christ, to spread the gospel, and to advance the kingdom of God.

3. A person who suffers greatly for being a Christian.

There are those who say a Christian cannot be a martyr for Jesus Christ unless they are killed for Him. But if given the choice of being killed quickly or enduring imprisonment, torture and constant pain for months and years – and perhaps being crippled and in pain for the rest of your life as a result – which would you choose? Most of us would opt for the bullet every time. Oftentimes it takes far more faith, strength and courage to endure long-term suffering and pain.

Whether a Christian dies quickly or suffers for weeks, months or years as a witness for Jesus Christ — or just for being a Christian — their name is written in the book of martyrs in heaven along with the names of Stephen, James, Paul, Peter, Timothy and all the other great heroes of our faith.

An incredible picture of a Christian martyr is found in the following two statements.

As a communist officer beat a young Christian, he said, "I am almighty as you believe your God to be. I have the power to kill you!"

Through his pain, the Christian replied, "God's almighty power is all on my side. I can love you while you torture me to death."

Jesus of Nazareth

Jerusalem circa AD 27

It all began with Jesus of Nazareth.

When He was twelve years old, Jesus made a statement that became the focus of His life and pointed toward a hill called Calvary. Luke wrote in his Gospel that every year during the Feast of the Passover, Jesus and His parents went to Jerusalem. It was no different when Jesus was twelve. This year, however, something unusual did happen.

When the days of Passover were completed, Mary and Joseph began the journey back to Nazareth. They didn't realize that young Jesus had lingered at the temple in Jerusalem. Supposing Jesus to be in the traveling company, they went a day's journey before they sought Him among their relatives and acquaintances. When they discovered that He wasn't with them, they returned to Jerusalem to find Him.

Now so it was that after three days they found Him in the temple, sitting in the midst of the teachers, both listening to them and asking them questions. And all who heard Him were astonished at His understanding and answers.

So when they saw Him, they were amazed; and His mother said to Him, "Son, why have You done this to us? Look, Your father and I have sought You anxiously."

And He said to them, *"Why did you seek Me? Did you not know that I must be about My Father's business?"* Luke 2:46-50

Ever since then, every martyred Christian, from the youngest to the oldest, has been martyred while being about their Father's business. They were living their lives as Christians in the midst of a dark world, putting their lives in harm's way for the cause of Jesus Christ 3/4 just like some of the students at Columbine High School in Littleton, Colorado, USA 1999.

Cassie Bernall
United States 1999

The early Christians counted it all joy when they were found worthy to suffer for Jesus. Cassie Bernall's moment of ultimate worth came when an ordinary school day turned into an extraordinary moment of United States history. With a gun pointed at her head, one of her fellow students asked, "Do you believe in God?"

The enraged shooter's finger pressed on the trigger, and Cassie had only a few seconds of life left regardless of her answer. There was no time to think about an answer, but Cassie did not have to think. God was so much a part of her life, of her heart and soul. She had made her eternal commitment long before this moment of truth, and her answer came quickly and naturally.

"Yes, I believe in God!"

"Why?" asked the shooter. Then he pulled the trigger before she could reply — almost as if he was afraid of her answer. Not long after that, he shot himself. In less than a heartbeat he knew the answer to his question to Cassie.

Unfortunately, the answer came too late.

Rachel Scott

United States 1999

Someone who knew her said that Rachel Scott was an actor, a clown, a girl who wore sunglasses to the prom and once stuffed twenty-four marshmallows into her cheeks to win a "Chubby Bunny" contest. A Columbine High School teacher said, "She shined. She shined for God at all times. She made a choice to love life."

Rachel loved life because above everything and everyone else she had chosen to love God – the Lord of life – first and foremost. In one of her journal entries, she wrote:

I lost all my friends at school. Now that I
have begun to walk my talk, they make fun of
me. I don't even know what I have done. I
don't really have to say anything, and they
turn me away.
I have no more personal friends at school. . .
. But it's all worth it to me. I am not going to
apologize for speaking the name of Jesus, I
am not going to justify my faith to them, and I
am not going to hide the light that God has
put into me.
If I have to sacrifice everything . . . I will. I
will take it. If my friends have to become my
enemies for me to be with my best friend,
Jesus, then that's fine with me.
I always knew that part of being a Christian
is having enemies . . . but I never thought that
my "friends" were going to be those enemies.

In another journal entry, Rachel asked this
question of God: "Why can't I be used by You?"
Though she did not seem to realize it, she was being
used every day. Soon, she would be used in a way that
would tie her name tightly together with that of God
and Jesus Christ throughout the world.

In one of her journals, Rachel wrote

I am nothing
I have nothing
People pass by me
And nod their head

And extend their hand.
People pass by me
But never do they stop
I am nothing
I have nothing.

Rachel had no way of knowing that because of her love for and dedication to Jesus Christ, she would be more and have more than she ever imagined or dreamed! Nor would she know until she stood in glory before the Lord she loved so much that it would take a mad killer's bullet to make her dream come true—to make her a shining example of love for Jesus to hundreds of thousands all over the world.

Stephen
Israel circa AD 35

Stephen, whose name means "crown," was the first person to be killed because he was a Christian. He was still a young man at the time of his death.

In Acts, chapter 6, we learn that Stephen wasn't a leader in the Church, he was a table waiter who made certain the food was distributed equally every day. The Apostles did not want to leave their prayers and study of the Word to serve tables, so they instructed the people to choose seven men who had good reputations and were full of the Holy Spirit. These men would take care of the food distribution.

Stephen was one of the seven who was chosen. He was not only full of the Holy Spirit, but he was also full of faith and power. He prayed for the needs of the people, especially the sick, as he distributed food. He testified about Jesus, and it wasn't long before everybody began to notice that people got healed when Stephen prayed for them. This made him extremely popular with the Christians — and extremely unpopular with those who were against this new Way.

To stop Stephen, his enemies persuaded some men to say that he was speaking blasphemous words against Moses and God. This stirred up the Jewish people and their leaders. They seized Stephen and brought him before their religious council. Witnesses lied and said that Stephen was not only saying blasphemous things against Moses and God, but also against the holy temple and the law. They swore that he had also said that Jesus of Nazareth was going to destroy the temple and change all the customs they had received from Moses.

All through these accusations, Stephen sat quietly. The Bible says that when they looked at him, his face looked like the face of an angel. When the high priest asked Stephen if the things said about him were true, Stephen boldly recounted the entire history of their ancestors' dealings with God, starting with Abraham. He told the council members all God had done for them even though they had resisted Him through the generations. He ended with this powerful statement:

"You stiff-necked people, with uncircumcised hearts and ears! You are just like your fathers: You always resist the Holy Spirit! Was there ever a prophet your fathers did not persecute? They even killed those who predicted the coming of the Righteous One. And now you have betrayed and murdered him — you who have received the law that was put into effect through angels but have not obeyed it."

Acts 7:51-53

The council members were so furious when they heard this, the Bible says that they gnashed their teeth at him. It goes on to say:

But Stephen, full of the Holy Spirit, looked up to heaven and saw the glory of God, and Jesus standing at the right hand of God. 'Look," he said, "I see heaven open and the Son of Man standing at the right hand of God."

Acts 7:55-56

When Stephen said this, the council's anger turned to rage because the "right hand of God" represents the power of God. For Stephen to say that Jesus was standing at the right hand of God was to say that He was judging them with the power and authority of God. (It is interesting that many years ago, and still in some countries today, the judge — or judges — stood when passing sentence on the accused. In the United States it has been reversed, and the accused stands while sentence is passed.)

At this they covered their ears and, yelling at the top of their voices, they all rushed at him, dragged him out of the city and began to stone him.

Acts 7:57-58

Imagine the scene. Stephen is dragged to the stoning place. All his clothes except his loincloth are torn from him. He is thrown into the middle of a circle of furious, screaming men, who are calling him every possible derogatory, religious name. Rocks of all shapes and sizes are piled at their feet. Some pick up the sharpest rocks they can throw with one hand, some wield larger rocks they can only throw with two hands.

Stephen looks around the circle. He sees a man holding the cloaks of his executioners. The man is Saul of Tarsus, a well-known persecutor of the Way. Then Stephen looks for just one friendly face to strengthen him. There is none.

The first rocks are thrown at his back. They knock him forward. Then rocks begin to strike his head, chest, stomach and legs. He looks upward and prays, "Lord Jesus, receive my spirit."

More rocks than can be counted are being hurled at him. They crash into his body, and he feels excruciating pain as his bones crack and break. He staggers blindly as rocks tear out his eyes. He is covered with blood and struggles to stand, but falls to his knees and cries out, "Lord, do not hold this sin against them." His hands stretch out for a moment as if to touch someone, and then he falls slowly forward and dies.

His executioners silently stare at his still body as two of them make certain he's dead. When the examiners nod their heads, they drop the rocks in their hands and smile grimly. They gather their cloaks from Saul and head toward the city, returning to their homes and the holy temple.

Abuk
Sudan 1995

Abuk lives in the war-ravaged country of Sudan, where a jihad, or Islamic holy war, has raged for over twenty years against the predominantly Christian south.

At the time of the atrocity, Abuk lived with her family in a small village near the front lines of battle. One morning just after dawn, Islamic soldiers raided her village. Most of the villagers fled before the rampaging soldiers, but Abuk was not able to get away in time. Several soldiers seized her and told her that she had to go with them. She refused.

They told her, "You must stop being a Christian and become a Muslim. You must renounce this Jesus and accept Mohammed as the chief and last prophet of God!" Abuk refused again.

Enraged at her refusals, the soldiers savagely tore off her clothes and tied her up. They started a fire and put their large knives into it. When the knives were red hot, they removed them from the fire and stabbed, sliced, and mutilated Abuk's upper chest, shoulders and back.

Fighting to hold back her screams of pain, Abuk prayed to Jesus for the strength to withstand the agonizing torture and not deny Him. "Jesus, help me and make me strong!" she cried.

When Abuk still refused to renounce Jesus Christ, the soldiers beat her until she was unconscious and left her to die of her wounds. Sometime later, she regained consciousness. Stumbling, falling and often crawling, she made her way to the other villagers to get help.

Though it has been several years since she was tortured for her refusal to renounce Jesus, Abuk still suffers from her massive wounds. The scars are often infected, and she is in almost constant pain because of a lack of proper medical help.

Abuk still has strong faith in Jesus Christ, and has said she would suffer again for Him. She is always strengthened when Christians come to her village to bring supplies, to encourage them, and to tell them that their brothers and sisters in Christ throughout the world are praying for them.

Blandina and Ponticus
Roman Empire circa AD 175

Blandina was a frail Christian girl. No one thought she would be able to resist physical torture, but her inner strength was so great that the men who tortured her actually wore themselves out trying to get her to renounce Jesus Christ. Finally they gave up and took her to an amphitheater, like the coliseum in Rome. They hung her and three others on a piece of wood stuck into the ground. They were to be food for hungry, wild lions that were kept in cages beneath the amphitheater.

While waiting for the lions to be released, Blandina prayed earnestly for her companions and encouraged them. But none of the lions would touch her, although they killed and ate the other three. She was put back into prison.

This happened twice!

The last time Blandina was brought out, she was accompanied by fifteen-year-old Ponticus. Ponticus had only been a Christian for a short time, but his faith in Jesus Christ was extremely strong. He had already refused to renounce Jesus even though he had been cruelly tortured.

As they entered the amphitheater together, they continually encouraged and prayed for each other. The combined strength and steadfastness of their faith so enraged their tormentors and the screaming, hate-filled, multitude that neither her sex nor his youth were respected. They were subjected to the severest torture.

Blandina was torn by the lions, scourged like Jesus was, put into a net and tossed about by a wild bull, and placed naked into a red-hot metal chair. When she was able to talk, she encouraged all the Christians near her to hold fast to their faith in Jesus. "Do not renounce your Lord," she said, "for you will soon be with Him in Paradise."

Ponticus was tortured so severely that he passed out several times. But each time he came to, he praised Jesus and shouted encouragement to the others. "Praise Jesus, we are going to be with Him!" Like Blandina, Ponticus held fast to his faith until he died from the pain.

Blandina's torturers were determined to make her renounce her faith in Jesus. When they could not, and she was so far gone that she could barely moan, they gave up and killed her with a sword.

Kamerino
Sudan 2000

Fundamentalist Muslim forces had been roaming the area around the small village for days, and the Christian villagers were afraid to leave their homes even to get food. Ten-year-old Kamerino hadn't eaten for many days. The hunger pains had stopped, and he knew that if he did not get food for himself and his grandmother soon, they would starve to death.

The Islamic army had killed his parents, and now there was a good chance that they would kill him if he went out. But what choice did he have? So he and three close friends made plans to go out early the next morning and search for food.

His grandmother reluctantly agreed to let him go. "You must be very careful, Kamerino, and you must promise me that you and your friends will be back before the day is over." Kamerino promised.

The four boys left just after dawn the next morning. But in their desperate search for food, they were careless and ran into a large group of Islamic soldiers. A Muslim officer yelled at the boys, "Stop! Come here to me!"

Fearing for their lives, of being sold as slaves or made Muslims, the boys ran into a small, nearby field and hid in the tall grass. They remained silent and stayed low as the soldiers searched through the grass, yelling, "If you come out, we will not harm you. But if you do not come out we will kill you when we find you!"

When they heard the soldiers leave the field, the boys hoped they had given up and gone away. But the soldiers were enraged at the thought of four small boys outwitting them, so they surrounded the small field and set it on fire. "You must come out now," they yelled, "or you will burn to death!"

As the flames encircled the field and burned toward them, the boys kept moving toward the center of the field. Eventually the circle of fire was too close. Three of the boys ran out of the field as rapidly as they could, hoping to dodge the soldiers and get away. But it was no use. They were quickly and easily caught. Their fate was sealed, whether it was to be killed, to be made slaves or to become Muslims.

Kamerino chose to stay in the field, curling himself up into a small ball as the fire consumed him. After the field burned to the ground, the Muslim soldiers searched the scorched ground for the fourth boy. They found Kamerino's motionless body curled up on the ground, burned from head to toe.

"He's dead," one of the officers said. "Leave him there as a warning to others." Herding their three young prisoners ahead of them like cattle, they left the area.

Several days later, a missionary team bringing blankets and other items to the southern Sudanese Christians drove north to the village of Kit, just fifty miles from the Islamic front. That evening they showed the Jesus film, distributed most of their supplies, and started the trip back the next morning.

A few miles outside Kit they came upon a Sudanese military camp and stopped to distribute some blankets to the wives and children of the soldiers who were fighting on the front lines. Then they sat down for a few moments to talk to some of the military officers.

While they were talking, a Sudanese woman tapped one of the team members on the shoulder and said, "Please come quickly. Please come to see this little boy. He has skin problems."

Not certain of what the pleading women meant by "skin problems," the team members followed the woman into a tiny room in a small cement structure. There were no lights or windows in the room, so one of them turned on his flashlight and began shining it along the floor. On one side of the room they saw a young boy lying on the cement floor on a small, green, piece of plastic. His body was covered with a tattered blanket. He stared up into the beam of light with pain-filled eyes, but did not make a sound.

They smelled burnt flesh as two of the team members knelt next to the boy and gently lifted the blanket. Hundreds of flies covered his body and hovered around the room. His skin was blistered and cracked. A purple dye stained parts of his body where someone had vainly tried to treat his burns. It was Kamerino. God's grace had brought them to him.

When Kamerino had not returned to the village with his friends that day, his grandmother had asked some of the villagers to go out and search for him. They had found him trying to get home. Somehow he had managed to get to his feet and make his way back to the village after the Islamic soldiers had left. He hadn't walked very far before the villagers found him. His chest was so badly burned that he had trouble breathing, and his feet were so deeply burned that they could hardly bear the weight of his small body.

The villagers carried Kamerino back to the village, put him in the small room, and left him to whatever treatment his grandmother could give him. It would take every ounce of his strength and will to survive. The villagers had little hope that he would live, for they had no way to transport him to the Christian hospital in Nimule, which was nearly fifty miles south of them.

When the missionary team arrived, it had been eight days since the Islamic soldiers had set the field on fire and burned Kamerino nearly to death. After being told what happened to Kamerino, the team members rearranged their belongings in the truck, grabbed the green plastic by the corners, lifted the boy into the truck bed and secured him as well as they could. They assured Kamerino's grandmother that they were taking her grandson to the hospital to get proper medical treatment.

Able to understand and speak only a little English, and confused by the speed with which everything was happening, Kamerino was too scared to talk. Every time the truck hit a rough spot in the road, however, he would scream. Unfortunately, the road to Nimule was crude and the truck constantly bounced and rolled back and forth.

The Sudan is filled with death and suffering. Thousands die yearly at the hands of the Islamic army or from disease and starvation. But the only thought in the minds of those in the truck was getting the young Sudanese boy to the safety and care of the Nimule Christian hospital.

Finally arriving at the hospital, Kamerino was gently lifted out of the truck bed and placed upon a stretcher by Christian nurses. They quickly carried him in to begin his treatment. Understanding where he was, Kamerino said as loud and as well as he could to his rescuers, "Thank you for helping me"

Today Kamerino is well on his way to complete recovery, but like many who suffered for Jesus throughout the history of the Church, he will always bear in his body the marks of persecution. An inquiry to the Voice of the Martyrs about his present circumstances brought back this reply.

Kamerino is now living in an orphanage and has been assigned to the care of a Christian lady there. We praise God that she is a Christian. He says that when he is older he wants to go and try to find his relatives so he can be with his family again. In the horrible tragedies of that country so many families are separated. We are praying that one day Kamerino will be united with his family members and relatives that are still alive.

Perpetua, Felicitas and Revocatus of Carthage

Roman Empire circa AD 200

Perpetua was a young married woman who was still nursing a child. When she was arrested, she was with a young pregnant woman, Felicitas, and Revocatus of Carthage, a slave who was being taught the principles of Christianity.

Perpetua stood before the proconsul, Minutius. He offered her freedom if she sacrificed to Roman idols, but she refused. So they took her nursing baby from her and threw her into a dungeon filled with other Christians — some not yet in their teens and others in their eighties.

Describing her faith and life in prison, Perpetua told her father, " The dungeon is to me a palace." Later she and the other prisoners appeared before Hilarianus, the judge. He also offered to set her free if she would sacrifice to the Roman idols. Her father was there with her baby and begged her to do so. She replied, "I will not sacrifice."

"Are you a Christian?" asked Hilarianus.

"I am a Christian," Perpetua replied.

All of the Christians with her stood fast for Jesus. They were ordered to be killed by wild beasts for the enjoyment of the crowd on the next pagan holiday. The men were to be torn by lions and leopards and the women set upon by bulls.

On the day of their execution, Perpetua and Felicitas were first stripped naked and hung in nets. However, the crowd objected to their being naked, so they were removed to be clothed before the torture began. When Perpetua and Felicitas were brought back into the arena, a wild bull was set upon them. Perpetua was tossed several times. She was stunned by the impact, but not seriously hurt.

Felicitas, however, was badly gored. When she was able, Perpetua hurried to her side and held her while they waited for the bull to charge them again. When the bull refused, they were dragged from the arena and led back to the dungeon, much to the crowd's disappointment.

After a few hours, they were brought back into the arena to be killed by gladiators. Felicitas was killed quickly by a scarred gladiator who looked as though he had fought many battles and took no pleasure in killing helpless women. But the young, inexperienced gladiator assigned to Perpetua trembled violently and could only stab her several times. Seeing how he trembled, Perpetua held his sword blade and guided it to a vital spot just under her left breast. "Thrust quickly and hard," she told him, "and may God forgive you." She made no further sound as the sword pierced her heart.

James Jeda

Sudan 1998

Nine-year-old James Jeda watched as Islamic soldiers killed his father, mother, and four brothers and sisters. Then they took him as a prisoner. He thought they were going to make him a slave, which was a common practice. So that evening when they told him to gather wood for a fire, he assumed they were getting ready to cook something for their supper.

When the fire was burning at its highest, the soldiers asked James if he had seen or heard of any rebel soldiers in the area. He told them he had not. Then they told him, "You must become a Muslim. Accept Mohammed as God's prophet and bow down to Allah."

Still in shock from seeing his parents and brothers and sisters killed, James told them with all the courage he could muster that he could not do that. "I am a Christian," he said, his voice trembling.

Angered by the young boy's refusal, the soldiers picked him up and threw him into the fire. "Then you will burn as a Christian!" they shouted at him.

They watched as the flames engulfed James, and when they did not see him moving they thought he had been knocked unconscious or had died of fright, so they packed up their weapons and left.

James wasn't dead, however. Somehow he withstood the terrible pain, and when the flames roared up around him he rolled out of them. He managed to run into the bush before the soldiers could see him.

Today the front of James's stomach is terribly scarred, and his right arm is partially deformed due to the heat of the fire. You can see the places on his body where the doctors have grafted skin over his third-degree burns. But his emotional pain is deeper than his physical scars. He still grieves over the death of his parents and brothers and sisters, and he feels the pain of being alone in the world. When you look into his eyes, you can see a young boy who has suffered things that most children never imagine or experience in their worst nightmares. Yet James has a ready, joyous smile, especially when he proudly proclaims, "I am a Christian."

Courageous Young Roman Women
Roman Empire circa AD 260

Rufina and Secunda were the beautiful and educated young daughters of a prominent man in Rome. They were engaged to two wealthy men, Armentarius and Verinus. All four were professed Christians.

When the persecutions began, however, the young men realized they were in danger of losing their money. They renounced their faith and tried to persuade the young ladies to do the same.

When the women would not, the gentlemen informed against them. Rufina and Secunda were arrested for being Christians and taken before the governor of Rome, Junius Donatus. He condemned them and sentenced them to be beheaded.

Three other Christian girls who lived near Rome were named Maxima, Donatilla and Secunda. They were still in their teens when they were condemned for refusing to reject Jesus as their Lord. For their faith, they were sentenced to be tortured and executed.

On the day their sentence was carried out, they were given gall and vinegar to drink. Perhaps this was to lessen their pain or to imitate how Jesus was offered gall and vinegar while He hung on the cross. They were horribly scourged and their wounds rubbed with lime. After that, they were hung and tortured on a gallows, scorched on a metal grid, torn by wild animals, and finally decapitated.

Zeba Masih

Pakistan 1999

Sharif Masih and his family lived in a small house on a farm. He rented it from the owners of the farm, where he worked for a yearly salary of only one hundred dollars. Each year he was forced to borrow money from his employers to provide enough food for his family. All of the other workers did the same.

The loans amounted to a form of legal slavery, because the workers were never able to pay even the principle on the loans. Therefore, they had to work for their employers for the rest of their lives. The only other payment Sharif received for his backbreaking work was fifty dollars worth of grain once a year.

Sharif had only daughters. His youngest, Zeba, was twelve and a Christian. To help with the family income, she agreed to take a job as a servant girl with a local Muslim family. Because she was a beautiful and sweet-spirited girl, Zeba's employers thought she would make a good wife for one of their young Muslim men.

In an attempt to convert Zeba to the Muslim faith, her employers attempted to teach her verses from the Koran, demanding that she memorize them. "I will not memorize anything from the Koran," Zeba told them, "I am a Christian."

Her employers and the other servants were furious that she did not comply with their requests, so they beat her with sticks and their fists, kicked her, and spat upon her. Then they had her arrested for crimes they said she committed against the state, but the charges were dismissed for lack of proof.

When Zeba's parents learned of the cruelty inflicted on their twelve-year-old daughter by her employers, Mrs. Masih rushed to their home to ask why they would harm her little girl. "What did she ever do to hurt you?" she asked. What happened to her as a result of her simple inquiry is almost unthinkable.

Mrs. Masih was beaten by Zeba's employers and their Muslim servants, then doused with gasoline and set on fire. Although she was rushed to the hospital by others who saw the incident, she died within a few hours. To add to the tragedy, Zeba's oldest sister, Aseema, was unable to bear the grief and hopelessness that had come upon her family. She went into shock and never recovered, literally dying of a broken heart a few weeks after her mother was killed.

After this senseless tragedy occurred, concerned Christians arranged to have Zeba trained in English, tailoring and business, so that she will never again be forced to work as a servant girl in a Muslim household. In addition, many Christians contributed money to pay off her father's debt to his employer so that he could find better employment for a higher wage.

"Then the King will say to those on His right hand, 'Come, you blessed of My Father, inherit the kingdom prepared for you from the foundation of the world: for I was hungry and you gave Me food; I was thirsty and you gave Me drink; I was a stranger and you took Me in;

I was naked and you clothed Me; I was sick and you visited Me; I was in prison and you came to Me.

"Then the righteous will answer Him, saying, 'Lord, when did we see You hungry and feed You, or thirsty and give You drink? 'When did we see You a stranger and take You in, or naked and clothe You? 'Or when did we see You sick, or in prison, and come to You?'

"And the King will answer and say to them, 'Assuredly, I say to you, inasmuch as you did it to one of the least of these My brethren, you did it to Me.'"

Matthew 25:34-40 NKJV

In Pakistan Christians are less than the lowest class of citizens. They are continually in danger, and Christians all over the world should lift them up in prayer every day.

Peter
Roman Empire circa AD 250

Peter was a young man from Rome who was well known for his superior intelligence and physical condition. He was an excellent student and an outstanding athlete. He was also a Christian.

Peter lived during the reign of the Roman Emperor Decius (AD 249-251), whose soldiers proclaimed him emperor against his will. His reign was noted for was severe persecution of Christians.

When it was learned by the authorities that Peter was a Christian, he was ordered to sacrifice to the goddess Venus. He refused. He was immediately arrested and brought before a tribunal headed by Optimus, the governor of Asia.

When the charge of refusing to sacrifice to the goddess Venus was read to Peter, he said, "I am amazed that you sacrifice to an infamous woman whose evil immoralities are recorded in your own writings and whose life consisted of such perverted actions that she would be arrested and punished by your own laws. No, I will not sacrifice to an evil and false goddess! I shall offer the true God the acceptable sacrifice of praises and prayers."

When Optimus heard this, he was so incensed that he sentenced Peter to be stretched upon a wheel until all his bones were broken and then to be beheaded. Some in the tribunal expected Peter to show fear and beg for his life rather than suffer such torture and pain, but instead he praised God that he was counted worthy to suffer for Jesus.

Maria Nenkeulah

Indonesia 2000

On the Indonesian Island of Haruku, a large number of Christian school children have lost one or both parents because of persecution. The children suffer as much or more from the persecution than their parents who died. Their intense sorrow and hardship classifies them as martyrs for their Christian faith.

One January night, fourteen-year-old Maria Nenkeulah grew worried when her mother and father had not returned home. Her parents had left her in charge of her younger brothers and sisters. "I waited for them until ten o'clock and wondered why they hadn't come back," Maria said. All night long she and the other children waited fearfully in the dark. They were afraid to go out and ask if anyone had seen their parents, but they were also afraid of knowing where they were.

The next day came and went, and still Maria's parents did not return home. She alerted other Christians in the village who began to search for them. After looking for them through that night and the next day, they found the bodies of Maria's parents buried beneath some banana leaves at the bottom of the village water well. They had been hacked to death by a radical Muslim mob.

Maria finds it difficult to forgive. She remains bitter against those responsible for killing her mother and father. "I still don't know whether I can forgive them or not because they have killed my parents. I still doubt about it."

Maria's six younger brothers and sisters were separated and are living with various relatives, because no single family could support them all. She asks Christians everywhere to pray for her. "Pray that God will give me the ability to eventually care for my brothers and sisters," she says. We must also pray that God will give her the grace to forgive those who so violently killed her mother and father.

Nichomachus and Denisa
Roman Empire circa 250

Nichomachus was a Christian who was brought before Optimus, the governor of Asia, and ordered to sacrifice to the pagan idols. By his words, Nichomachus seemed to be stronger than what others had thought. He said to Opitmus, "I cannot pay the respect to devils that is due only to the Almighty."

Opitmus flew into a rage and ordered Nichomachus to be placed on the rack. Nichomachus endured torment for only a short time before renouncing Jesus and telling his tormentors that he no longer believed that He was the Son of God. With that, they freed him from the rack.

Nichomachus staggered to his feet, stood upright for just a moment, and then screamed as if in great pain or fear. Suddenly he fell to the ground and died.

Among the observers was a sixteen-year-old girl named Denisa. She exclaimed, "O unhappy fool, why would you buy a moment's relief at the expense of a miserable eternity?" When Optimus heard of this, he called her before the council and asked her one question. "Are you a Christian?"

Denisa replied, "Yes, I am!"

"Then go to your dead Christ," Optimus said, and had her taken immediately to the dungeon and beheaded. In less time than it takes to say His name, Denisa was with Jesus — her Living Lord of Glory!

Atrocities on Kasiui Island
Indonesia 2000

One of the worst incidents in Indonesia occurred on the small island of Kasiui during the month of Ramadan, the Islamic holy month of fasting and prayer. Approximately one thousand armed radical Muslims, or jihad warriors, set out to persecute the local Christians.

On November 25th they began to burn homes. They rounded up nearly two hundred Christians and took them to a village mosque. When word reached the nearby villages, the Christians fled to the forest to protect their families. The jihad warriors continued their assault by burning homes, schools, and all the Bibles they could find.

The warriors then waited in hiding outside the destroyed villages for another five days until the Christian families, thinking they had left, came out of the forest. When they did, the armed Muslims surrounded them and forced them to the mosque where the other Christians were still being held.

During the assaults, seven Christian villagers were killed. Two schoolteachers were beheaded after seeking the protection of local Muslims who were thought to be more moderate. The head of one of the schoolteachers was put on a pole outside the mosque as a warning to the other Christians who were being held captive.

With approximately five hundred Christians now held captive, the jihad warriors proceeded to douse them with water to "cleanse" them in a Muslim ritual.

A fourteen-year-old girl, Marina, cried hysterically when she was doused with water. To her, this was symbolic of being purified in order to accept Islam, and she thought it meant she had renounced Jesus Christ. Later, Muslim women forcibly circumcised her.

After dousing the Christians with water, the armed Muslims surrounded them and began to recite Islamic prayers and verses from the Koran, demanding that the Christians recite them also. Those who refused were beaten and forced to stand in the hot sun in a nearby field for hours without food or water.

Next the Christians were forced back into the mosque, separated into groups to complete their "conversion" to Islam. They were told, "If you do not agree to be cut down below, we will cut you up above," referring to forced circumcisions of the men, women, and children. The Christians did not doubt the threats of the jihad warriors. They had only to look at the severed head of the local schoolteacher to know what they meant by "we will cut you up above."

The Christians were released from the mosque and sent home. Over a period of two days, the Muslims went from house to house and circumcised as many as ten Christians at a time with a single razorblade. No one was given antiseptic, painkillers, or bandages. A small piece of cotton was placed on the men's wounds only.

More women than men were circumcised, and even small children were cut. A six-year-old girl named Emiliana was restrained while she was forcibly butchered. She was too young and embarrassed to fully understand or talk about her experience. And too young to understand that her life was changed forever that day.

Before the assault was over, more than six hundred Christians, including fifty children, were forcibly circumcised. The victims were told they had to undergo circumcision if they were to be considered "real" Muslims. However, through the entire frightening and painful ordeal, not one of the six hundred Christian men, women and children renounced Jesus and became a Muslim.

The Christian Roman Legion
AD 286

In the year AD 286 there was a Roman Legion called the Theban Legion. Every soldier in this legion was a Christian — all six thousand, six hundred, and sixty-six of them. As was common in those days, many of them were still in their teens, most of them sons of legionnaires who were following in their fathers' footsteps.

They had been stationed in the east until the emperor Maximian ordered them to march to Gaul to assist him against the rebels of Burgundy. At that time Gaul was a region of western Europe where France and Belgium are today.

They traveled through the Alps under the command of Mauritius, Candidus and Exupernis, three highly respected officers. Every soldier in the Theban Legion would gladly follow them into battle, no matter what the odds were against them. At the end of their long journey, they joined with the forces of the emperor.

Soon after the Theban Legion arrived, Maximian ordered a general sacrifice to the Roman gods. The entire army was to assist. He also commanded them to take the oath of allegiance and swear to rid the Roman Empire of Christians. When the Theban Legion heard the emperor's orders, every soldier refused to sacrifice to false gods or to take the oath.

This so angered Maximian that he ordered the Theban Legion to be decimated — all the soldiers were to be lined up and every tenth soldier run through with a sword. The order was carried out, but those who were still alive did not waver in their determination to remain true to their Christian beliefs. So Maximian ordered a second decimation, and again every tenth soldier was killed.

This second slaughter did not deter the faith and perseverance of the soldiers any more than the first one had. They courageously held fast to their Christian beliefs. The Theban officers advised their men to draw up a statement of loyalty to their emperor, except in the matter of worship to Roman gods, and to protest the severity of his judgment on what were otherwise loyal soldiers.

Such a statement of loyalty would have softened and calmed down any normal person, but not Maximian! He went into a frenzy and commanded the entire legion to be put to death — all of the remaining 5,400 Christian soldiers. Accordingly, on September 22, 286 AD, Maximian's army raged through the Theban Legion and cut every one of them to pieces with their swords.

One can only imagine what it was like in heaven when 6,666 Christian Roman soldiers arrived in heaven and stood before their true Emperor Jesus, the King of Kings, no longer clothed in Roman armor, but now in robes of pure white, shining like the sun. What a sight it must have been!

Arsraf Masih

Pakistan 1997

Like many Christian parents all over the world, Ashraf Masih and his wife sent their fifteen-year-old son, whom we'll call Jara, off to school one day. And, like all those parents, they expected their young son to come home after school. But he did not. When it was past time for him to be home, Ashraf went to the school, but there was no sign of Jara. The next day passed and he was still missing. They continued to hunt for him through the remainder of the week, but without success, and the Islamic military authorities would not help them.

That Sunday Ashraf and his family began to fast and pray for their son's return. Monday morning, he went to Jara's school and questioned his schoolmates. All of them said that they knew nothing about Jara's disappearance.

Ashraf and his wife were desperate. Then, while they were in prayer Tuesday morning, the Holy Spirit spoke to them, "Nothing is impossible for your Lord." Their burden lifted immediately, and they knew that somehow they would find Jara and bring him home.

On Wednesday one of Jara's teachers, a Muslim and a member of a military faction, offered to go with Ashraf to the Islamic military offices to try to get information about his son. There they learned that Jara was in a jihad camp, supposedly of his own free will. The jihad camps are training grounds for Islamic soldiers and terrorists. At the urging of Jara's teacher, the Islamic officials gave them directions to the camp and guaranteed them safe passage.

Accompanied by his other son and the Muslim teacher, Ashraf drove several miles from their town to a spot near the jihad camp, which was located near the top of a mountain. He parked the car and they climbed about half-a-mile to the camp. Ashraf was taken into a room and was told that Jara was in the room next to his. The camp commander, however, would not let Ashraf see him.

"He does not want to see you," the teacher said. "He is a Muslim now."

For two hours Ashraf begged to see his son. Finally the commander gave in. Ashraf did not know that Jara had been told under threat of death, "If your father tries to force you to go home, kill him and your brother." His jihad teachers were certain he was frightened enough to obey.

When Ashraf saw his son and the clothing he now wore, he collapsed in grief. Jara ran to him and threw his arms around him. Jara whispered in his father's ear, Jara said to him, "I want to leave this place. I only said I accepted Islam to save my life. I swear to you, Father, I never accepted it in my heart."

Ashraf then begged the camp commander to let him and his two sons return to their home. In a miracle of God's grace, the camp commander's heart softened. He allowed Ashraf, Jara and his brother to leave the camp. Once home, a joyful mother held in her arms a son she thought she had lost. Weeping with joy, they all praised God for his safe return.

Today Ashraf is a seminary student, and he often quotes the 23rd Psalm, "I have seen the valley of death." Yet even the valley of death did not dim his love for Jesus. He left two Bibles in the jihad camp, one for the commander and one for the Muslim teacher who helped him to find his son.

Zia Nodrat

Afghanistan circa 1970

A wise Christian once said, "Fulfill the will of God with a smile, even if it means pain." This wisdom is illustrated valiantly by many persecuted Christians all over the world on a daily basis, but one particular incident in Afghanistan stands out.

One day the Muslim government sent workmen with bulldozers to destroy the only Christian church in Kabul, the capital of Afghanistan. The workmen expected the Christians to oppose them violently, but instead they were given tea and cookies! The workers destroyed the church anyway, but the compassion of Jesus proved much stronger in the Christians of Afghanistan.

Zia, a blind Afghan boy, was fourteen years old when he received Jesus Christ as his Lord and Savior. He was immediately warned that Mohammed's law decrees death for anyone who leaves Islam. Zia replied, "I have counted the cost and am willing to die for the Savior, since He has died on the cross for me." After Zia completed his schooling, he translated the New Testament into his own language and had it published.

When the Communists took over the country, Zia, who was now a pastor, was jailed and obliged to sleep on the freezing floor. Clothed in only a jacket and an overcoat, he met another Christian prisoner who did not have a jacket. Remembering the words of John the Baptist, "The one who has two tunics should share with the one who has none," he gave his coat to the other prisoner.

Zia said, "After I gave him my coat, I felt warmer and slept better than before."

During his time in the Afghanistan prison, Zia was tortured with electric shocks, which left burn marks all over his body. Eventually he was released and went to Pakistan, where he started an institute for the blind and preached to the Muslims. In March 1988 he was kidnapped by a fanatical Muslim group. Eyewitnesses saw the Muslims beat him with iron rods for hours, even after he lost consciousness. He was never seen again, and his body was never found.

Zia not only gave up his overcoat for Jesus. He gave up his life.

Rachela
Nigeria 1998

The Gbagri in Nigeria wanted a piece of land that was inhabited mostly by Christians. So in 1998 the predominantly Muslim Gbagri raiders attacked sixteen-year-old Rachela's village. Their goal was to scare Rachela and her tribe off their land.

"The first time the village was attacked," Rachela said, "my family all ran off into the bush and hid for several days. When Sunday came, my father said we should return to the village to go to church. On Sundays Muslims come to the village and check the people in church, but father insisted that we go, so we obeyed.

"While we were in church, the Muslims did come, and as we left they attacked us. We ran for our lives, but father became tired and fell. He was quickly surrounded by Muslims and they shot him. He died right there on the ground."

Sixty-eight churches were attacked that Sunday morning. The attacks were timed to coincide with the end of the church services. Electric generators and any other usable materials were stolen, and then many of the churches were burned.

Later that night some Christians returned to the village and found the body of Rachela's father, still lying in the path where he had been murdered. They buried him immediately to prevent the Muslims from coming back and burning his body. The rest of Rachela's family remained hidden in the bush.

"We heard of the burial of our father," Rachela said," but since we have not seen him since he fell, we cannot mourn him as we should."

Rachela's family fled their village, traveling on foot to another town for refuge. They walked for many days, surviving by eating flying ants. "Since then," Rachela said, "we have been wandering around in a daze. We are so shocked by what has happened. We don't think about our returning to school, just finding a safe place."

Rachela's family is now separated. Her mother and the other children stay in one village with relatives, and Rachela is in a different village with other relatives. What they are not separated from, however, is their faith in Jesus Christ. The persecution they have experienced has only strengthened their love for Him.

Eulalia

December AD 303

Eulalia was a young Christian Spanish girl, born and raised by Christian parents. In her childhood and throughout her early teens she was considered remarkable for her pleasing personality, sweet disposition, and the depth of her understanding of people, life, and especially her Christian faith.

When the authorities learned that she was a Christian and was talking to other young people about Jesus, they had her arrested and brought before the local Roman magistrate. Using what he considered effective persuasion, the magistrate tried to bring Eulalia over to paganism and the worship of the Roman gods. When he could not, he threatened her with severe punishment — punishment in keeping with her young age.

In the face of the threat of punishment, Eulalia not only refused, but she ridiculed Rome's pagan gods. She was so effective that the magistrate became enraged and ordered her to be tortured without mercy.

Eulalia was immediately taken to the prison dungeon, and there her sides were torn with hooks. Her upper body was burned so deeply with torches that she died during the torture — praising Jesus that she was counted worthy to suffer for Him.

Abraham

Sudan 1998

Abraham was a young Sudanese pastor who had started a church in the southern district of war-torn Sudan. It had grown to over four hundred active members, including many young people and children. Like many congregations in the Sudan, the church members had no Bibles. There was only one ragged and worn, red-covered New Testament.

The spiritual life and growth of Abraham's church members centered on that book. It was very precious to them, but especially to Abraham. That New Testament was how God had brought him to Jesus Christ. The red-covered book had been given to him many years before by some young people on an outreach mission to the Sudan. They had tried to witness to Abraham and his family, but he had not responded to the gospel. He had, however, kept the New Testament they had given him.

In the months following, he read the New Testament through again and again. After about a year, he gave himself and his life to Jesus. Not long after his salvation, he felt that God was calling him to the ministry, so he left home to attend a seminary. When he finished his schooling, he returned to his village and began building a church, person by person and heart by heart.

In Sudan, where civil war had ravaged the people and the land for over twenty years, it wasn't easy or safe to be a Christian, not to mention a pastor.

Sudan's Islamic government was on a mission to convert every person in the country to Islam. Those who wouldn't convert were beaten, tortured and often killed. Churches were burned time and again, some with the Christians still inside them.

Young women and teenage girls were forced to be Islamic concubines. Young boys were sold as slaves. Others were sent to Muslim schools where they were forced to memorize the Koran in Arabic, which takes seven to nine years. André is a survivor of a Christian church destroyed by fire in Sudan. His entire back and left arm were badly burned.

André says, "I was praying in our church with ninety-nine other believers. The Islamic government soldiers came and bolted the doors of our church shut. Then they set the church on fire. We could not escape. I crawled under the bodies of my brothers and sisters [in Christ] who had fallen to the floor from the smoke and flames and hid there. The soldiers kept watching until the church burned to the ground and then left us all for dead. I was the only one who survived."

In the midst of all this danger and persecution, Pastor Abraham labored for the Lord, shepherding his flock literally in the valley of the shadow of death. Yet he did it with a joyous smile and a warm heart.

Then one day Islamic government soldiers rode into his village on horseback and opened fire on men, women and children. They looted, burned and killed, leaving as quickly as they had come. Just four days prior to their attack, an organization that ministers to the persecuted church had brought a supply of Bibles in the Dinka language for Pastor

Abraham's congregation — the first they had ever had. But the soldiers burned them all, including Abraham's ragged New Testament.

As they went through the debris after the bloody attack, members of Pastor Abraham's church found his bullet-riddled body. Although he has gone to be with the Lord, his congregation lives on and flourishes, a tribute to the courage and faith of a young pastor and his worn, red-covered New Testament — a New Testament that was given to him by a youth group — a youth group who may never know until they get to heaven what their work for Jesus accomplished in the heart and soul of Abraham and the members of his congregation.

Hermenigildus
Spain AD 586

Hermenigildus was the oldest son of Leovigildus, a king of the Goths. Originally an Arian, he was converted to orthodox Christian faith by his godly wife, Ingonda. The Arians denied that Jesus was of the same substance as God. They believed that He was only the highest of created beings. They were violently opposed to those who were orthodox Christian believers — those who believed all that the Bible said about Jesus of Nazareth.

When Hermenigildus' father heard that he no longer believed the way the Arians believed, he removed Hermenigildus as governor of Seville in southwest Spain. He also threatened to execute him unless he recanted his belief in Jesus as the Son of God. To prevent his execution, Hermenigildus gathered an army of orthodox Christian believers who would fight with him.

In response to his son's rebellion, Leovigildus began to persecute all true believers in Jesus Christ. He also led a powerful army toward Seville, where his son had gathered his forces. At first Hermenigildus took refuge in Seville itself, but when his father's army overwhelmed his Christian forces, he fled to Asieta [city unknown], where he was captured after a short battle.

Encased in so many chains that only his head, hands and feet could be seen, Hermenigildus was taken back to Seville. Not long after, at the feast of

Easter, he was brought before an Arian bishop and ordered to receive the communion host. He refused to take it, saying, "For me to receive this bread from the hands of an unbeliever would be to deny that Jesus is the Son of God."

Hearing this, his father commanded his son's guards to immediately cut him to pieces with their swords. On April 13, 586, Hermenigildus went to be with the Son of God in glory.

Roy Pontoh
Indonesia 1999

In January of 1999 Christian children and teenagers attended a Bible camp at Pattimura University, which is on the island of Ambon, Indonesia. When the camp was over, cars were to take the laughing, rejoicing young people and children back to their homes, but there were many of them and not enough cars. So Pastor Mecky Sainyakit and three other Christian men left for Wakal village to rent more transportation.

On their way to the village, they were stopped by a mob of Muslims, who pulled them from their car and attacked them. Pastor Mecky and one of the other men were stabbed to death. The other two men escaped. The raging mob then burned the bodies of the two Christian men they had brutally murdered.

Back in the Bible camp at the University, the young people and children became frightened when they heard shouts of death and Muslim chants coming toward them. They rushed around trying to find hiding places, but when the mob reached the University they forced many of them out into the open. One of them was fifteen-year-old Roy Pontoh.

Roy was terribly frightened and trembling, but not so much that he would renounce his faith in Jesus Christ. When the Muslim mob threatened to kill him if he did not renounce Christianity and become a Muslim and soldier of Allah, the teenager refused. He mustered all the courage he had, and with a quivering voice declared, "I am a soldier of Christ."

Hearing those words, an enraged Muslim attacker swung his sword at Roy's stomach. He knocked the Bible out of his hands, which Roy had held out in front of him as a testimony of his faith. The soldier swung his sword again and sliced through Roy's stomach, cutting it open from side to side. Roy fell backwards, clutching his middle. He uttered one final word just before he died, "Jesus."

The mob dragged Roy's body away and threw it into a ditch, like it was the body of a dead animal. Four days later his family found his body and took it home. They gave Roy a Christian burial. Although often torn by grief, Roy's Christian parents are proud that their young son stood firm and strong in his faith in Jesus Christ. And they know that he is with the Lord that he loved so much, he would not deny

Kiffien

Germany AD 689

Kiffien was born in Ireland and was given a Christ-centered Christian education by his godly parents. While a young man he obtained a license from the Roman pope to preach to the pagans in Franconia in Germany.

At Wurzburg, which is a city in Bavaria on the Main River, sixty miles (or one hundred kilometers) southeast of Frankfurt, he converted the governor, Gozbert. Gozbert's Christianity was so godly that over a period of two years it inspired most of the citizens of that town to convert also.

In AD 689, Kiffien convinced the governor, who was married to his brother's widow, that the marriage was sinful, whereupon the widow had him beheaded before the governor could stop her.

Debbie

Egypt circa 1997

The Coptic Church is the Christian church of Egypt. They adhere to the Monophysite doctrine, which means that Jesus possessed a single divine nature, instead of having both a human nature and divine nature. Coptic and Syrian Christians profess this doctrine.

Debbie was a Coptic Christian who attended an Egyptian university. While she was there, two Muslim girls became extremely friendly with her and did everything they could to make her feel comfortable around them. For the first year of their friendship, they did not speak about religion at all.

During the second year, the two girls began to make offhand remarks about Islam. Whenever one of them made a remark, the other one would hush her and say that they had to respect Debbie's religious beliefs. All this pleased Debbie, and she gradually began to trust her Muslim friends more and more. When they invited her to go on a trip with them, she eagerly accepted. A second trip soon followed, and the Muslim girls began to bring up the subject of Islam more often.

Then one day the girls told Debbie they were going to a secluded place to contemplate and invited her to go with them. Still trusting them, Debbie went. When they arrived, she realized that the secluded place of contemplation was a home where Christian girls convert to Islam.

Debbie became quite nervous and told her friends that she had to return home immediately. But they convinced her to spend one night in the home, telling her they wanted to spend the night in contemplation. However, the next day when Debbie tried to leave, she discovered that the front and back doors of the home were locked. She was trapped inside.

Each day Debbie was forced to listen to a Muslim professor who taught about Islam. The pressure to give up Christianity and convert to Islam was weak at first, but it quickly became more forceful. Finally Debbie agreed to cover her head with a "hijab," a scarf-like cloth that is wrapped around the head.

There were five "conversion" teams in the home, each with a specific work. The work of the first team was to teach the girls about Islam and pressure them to convert. The second team guarded the girls so they would not escape from the house before they converted. The third team tempted the girls with things that were sins for Christians, which would supposedly prove to them that they weren't Christians at all. The fourth team threatened the girls and tried to frighten them into converting to Islam. They told them that anyone who leaves Islam is to be killed. This team told Debbie that she had already converted and she knew too much. She would never be allowed to leave the home and reveal all she had learned.

The work of the fifth team was sexual assault. They told the girls that if they refused to convert they would be sexually assaulted by a Muslim man and forced to marry him. In Egypt, as in many Muslim countries, being sexually assaulted is shameful for the victim and her family. It's almost impossible for a girl who has been sexually molested to find a husband, so she is often pressured into marrying the very man who assaulted her! That may be the only way she will ever marry, and marrying her molester will prevent shame from coming on her family.

Debbie spent eight weeks in the conversion home. During that time she decided to reverse the roles and win the trust of her captors. She did just that by chanting verses from the Koran and taking part in Muslim prayers — but only with her mouth and not in her heart. Because they had kidnapped her and she had been such a tough case in the beginning, the leaders of the home celebrated her supposed conversion. They even gave her a key to the front door!

Two weeks after the celebration, at four in the morning Debbie sneaked out of the home and escaped. She made her way to a Christian leader she knew, who helped her find her family. They had been searching everywhere for her and had been unable to get any help from the local police.

Debbie said that while she was held prisoner, she learned that there were many conversion homes as well as teams working in the universities in Egypt to coerce Christian girls into converting to Islam. Though their names will never be known, all Christian girls in Egypt need their brothers and sisters in Christ to pray for their protection and for their faith to remain strong like Debbie's.

The Bamboo Curtain
China 196

An eyewitness report was received about the deaths of several Christians in a Communist labor camp.

In one instance, a young girl's hands and feet were bound and she was forced to kneel in the center of a circle of people. They were commanded to stone her or they would be shot. Several Christians refused and were immediately executed. But the girl died under a hail of stones — her face shining like that of Stephen in the book of Acts. Later, one of those who threw the stones broke down and received Jesus as his Lord and Savior.

In another account, a young man was hung on a cross like Jesus. During the six days before he died, he prayed constantly out loud that his persecutors would be forgiven and receive Jesus.

Another story tells of five students who were made to dig five deep holes. They were then put in the holes and other prisoners threw dirt on them. As they were buried alive they sang Christians hymns.

Faith in Jesus Christ is very strong in the Christians in China!

Raju
India 2000

Raju is a Christian in India. Here is his story in his own words.

"My Hindu name means 'servant of the god Shiva,' but by the amazing hand of the living God, at age thirteen I became a servant of the Lord Jesus. I come from a strong Hindu family living in a village near one of the most holy places for Hindus, famous for temples and pilgrim centers. In my village, most had never heard of Jesus.

"Everything went well with our family until we discovered that our mother had leprosy. The whole family became outcasts. For almost twenty years we went to many Hindu temples and spent a lot of money on treatment, but her condition only worsened.

"In utter hopelessness we moved to Bombay, hoping that in the huge city we might find better medical care. A Christian family that had experienced miracles of healing lived nearby. Seeing my mom, this family assured me that Jesus could help her. Because we were high-caste Hindus, my father wanted nothing to do with Jesus.

"My mother's condition gradually deteriorated. One day, in much agony, she consented to go to the Christian family. They said Jesus loved her unconditionally. She agreed to receive prayer. As soon as the believers prayed, she was healed of many other physical problems. Her leprosy, however, remained.

"Mom went to the Christian home whenever she could without my father discovering it. She was later healed completely. She began to tell others about the Jesus who healed her. My mother's life and ministry had a profound influence on me. I committed my life to the Lord, and He called me into the ministry.

"Later, when I was in the eighth grade, I had to stay in Bombay with my dad and older brother. They were angry that I had chosen to worship Jesus. Once they threw me out. I was on the street for ten days without food or shelter.

"When my dad and brother saw I wouldn't forsake Jesus, they let me come back. Then one day my brother and his friends decided they didn't want a Christian brother. They beat me with their fists and sticks and intended to kill me, but God saved my life.

"Just before Christmas 2000, my dad and older brother called me to visit them. I thought they wanted to have a friendly meeting, but they grabbed me and beat me up again. Then they officially disowned me of all family inheritance.

"I hope some day that my family will see Jesus' love in me and be saved."

Raju is now a pastor and church leader in India, despite continued persecution from his own family and other Hindus.

Perfectus
Spain AD 850

Perfectus was born in Corduba, Spain and raised in the Christian faith. He was highly intelligent and read any book he could get his hands on to gain knowledge. He was also known for his extreme piety. While still a young man, he was ordained a Roman priest and performed his duties far better than most men his age.

During this period of history most of Spain was dominated by the Muslims, who had defeated the Visigoths in AD 711. The Visigoths were members of the western Goths, who invaded the Roman Empire in the fourth century. and settled in France and Spain. They established a monarchy that lasted until the early eighth century, when they were defeated by the Muslims.

In AD 850 Perfectus spoke to a large gathering of people in Corduba's town square. He declared that Mohammed was an imposter, and soon after he was arrested and beheaded. Some courageous Christians obtained his body from the Muslims and gave him a Christian burial.

Scars of Faith

Sudan 1999

When VOM workers went to Sudan to interview Christians who had suffered persecution, their first interview was with a small group of boys who had been captured by Islamic soldiers. Their village had been attacked early in the morning. The villagers had tried to escape, but they had been quickly surrounded by soldiers.

The soldiers killed the elderly and the infants immediately. The boys watched as the Islamic soldiers plunged their swords into their friends and family members. After the slaughter, twenty-seven children, fourteen boys and thirteen girls, were rounded up and taken to a military camp about nine miles from the village. That evening, around seven o'clock, the boys were taken out of the camp's makeshift prison one at a time. Their hands and feet were tied together behind their backs and each was ordered to deny Jesus and become a Muslim. Each one refused.

The soldiers took red-hot coals from their cooking fire and piled them on the ground in front of the boys. When a boy refused to convert to Islam, a long stick was passed through his bound hands and feet, and he was held face down over the burning embers. Most of the boys passed out from the pain.

When the Muslims could not convince any of the boys to convert, they untied them and put them back in the prison enclosure. Later, they brought them all back out again, tied the hands and feet of the four youngest — who were between five and nine years old — and laid them in front of the other ten boys. While the other boys watched, they beat them with sticks.

All the younger boys had to do was accept the Muslim faith and the beating would stop. Not one of them did. They screamed from the beatings and yelled for their mothers, but not one of them was willing to become a Muslim. Each of the small boys held to their faith and gave up their life for Jesus Christ that night.

The older boys were tortured with fire again the next day, some with hands and feet tied in front of them and their backs exposed to the red-hot coals. But none of them renounced their faith in Jesus that day either. During the night, the soldiers became careless and all the boys managed to escape the enclosure. Eventually they were placed in the refugee camp, where the VOM workers found them. None of the boys knew what had happened to the thirteen young girls.

The boys who were interviewed had horrific scars on their stomachs or backs from the burning coals. They were asked what they would do if the Islamic soldiers captured them again and threatened their lives if they did not become Muslims. They all affirmed their faith in Jesus Christ and said they were willing to die if necessary.

Galia and Alexander

Soviet Union 1966

The following facts are from a copy of a letter written by Brother and Sister Slobda from Dubradi village to the Soviet premier, Aleksei Nikolayevich Kosygin. Kosygin was the Soviet premier who succeeded Nikita Khrushchev and presided over the former Soviet Union from 1964 to 1980.

The letter tells how a local communist court ordered the Slobda's daughter, Galia, who was eleven, and their son Alexander, who was nine, to be taken away because they had raised them in the Christian faith. For two years the children were kept in an atheistic boarding school that was so unsanitary, they were covered with lice. Galia's legs swelled to almost twice their size, and both children were sick with lung disease, possibly tuberculosis, on two occasions.

After two years of detention under these filthy conditions, the children ran away and made their way home. Soon after, the authorities came to the Slobda home to take the children back. Galia and Alexander climbed on a couch and wept terribly. Police officer Lebed, who came to the house, couldn't bear the cries of the children and left without them.

A few days later the children, who were of school age and required to attend school, left the house and went to school. The director of the school called Galia into his office. Police officer Lebed was waiting. He grabbed her and carried her out to a police car. She fought so hard that Lebed fell to the floor once, but he did not let go of her. Galia kept yelling, "Men, men, help!" But no one helped her.

Another Christian girl, Shura, was also thrown into the same car. She had been taken by the school nurse to the clinic to take some medicine. Other police officers were waiting there and captured her also. Neither child was returned to their parents.

After that, Alexander remained at home and was not sent to school.

Linh Dao

Vietnam circa 1995

Linh Dao's father was an underground church pastor in Vietnam. Linh was ten years old when four police officers burst into her home. Her father was forced to remain seated while the officers ransacked his home. They were searching for Bibles. Linh courageously had hidden some of the Bibles in her school knapsack. When the police asked about the contents of it, she simply said, "It is books for children." They did not even open it.

Nevertheless, Linh's father was arrested that day and sentenced to seven years of reeducation and hard labor. Word quickly spread about the arrest, and the neighborhood children began asking Linh about the criminal acts committed by her father. She told all of them that her father was not a criminal. He was a Christian and she was proud of him for not wavering in his faith!

Each day Linh made a mark on her wooden bookcase and prayed for her father. Each day her faith grew stronger as the Scriptures she studied took on a deeper meaning. After more than a year, Linh and her mother and sisters were allowed to visit her father in prison.

When they reached the compound, they were separated from him by a chainlink fence. But Linh found a small space in a gate and squeezed through it. She ran across the prison yard to her father and hugged him tightly. The guards watched her and, surprisingly, left her alone. They must have thought, "What harm can a little girl do?"

What they did not know was that Linh's mother had given her a pen to give to her father. In the days following he used that pen to write Scriptures and mini-sermons on cigarette paper. These cigarette sermons traveled from cell to cell and were instrumental in bringing many prisoners to Jesus.

Linh constantly prayed that her father would be able to preach the gospel in prison, and that he would be released early. Both prayers were answered. She is now a teenager and says, "Before my dad was in prison, I was just a child. I didn't need to worry about anything. It was a lot different after my dad left. I prayed every day and every night. My faith grew very fast. I knew one thing I had to concentrate on, and that was spending time learning from the Bible, so when I grew up I could be like my dad, sharing and preaching.

"It was a big surprise for me when I came home from school one day and saw my dad had been released from prison. I ran and gave him a big hug. We were very happy. I was proud of my family, and I wanted to yell and let the whole world know that I wasn't scared of anything — because God always protects each step I take in life."

Linh's faith grew while her dad was in prison, and she didn't wait until she grew up to share the gospel and to show that she was not afraid of persecution. As a youth leader for a homechurch, she has been taken to prison over fifteen times. "They questioned me all day for four to five days, from eight o'clock to five o'clock. They gave me no food and did not let me go to school. They wanted to know the names of the kids in the youth group, and why I was a member.

"It is a common thing to be questioned if you are on fire for God," she says. "My mother encouraged me during this time. She said it was a good opportunity to witness to the police."

Linh has this advice for young Christians in America. "Be willing and have an open heart. If you do, God will challenge you and give you things to do. He will bless you with everything He has. He has blessed me so much!"

Television? "We have television in Vietnam, but I am too busy to watch it."

Stanislus

Poland 1079

Bolislaus was the second king of Poland and was an outwardly pleasant man, but he had a tendency to be cruel. Over the years that cruel tendency began to control his life and reign, until he was publicly known for his sadistic actions against his own people.

Stanislus, who was bishop of Cracow, courageously took it upon himself to tell the king about his faults in a private conversation. He hoped that by so doing he could convince the king to stop his cruelties against his people.

Although Bolisluas freely admitted the monstrous evil of his crimes, he was infuriated that the bishop dared to chastise him for them every time they met — which was far too often for him. Tired of the unpleasant confrontations and having no intention of changing his actions, he looked for an opportunity to rid himself of the bishop, whose only crime was being faithful to his Christian duties.

One day Bolisluas heard that the bishop was alone in a nearby church, so he sent soldiers to kill him. They found Stanislus alone and were awed by his godly presence, so they were afraid to kill him. When they reported back to the king, he flew into a violent rage, snatched a knife from one of them and raced to the chapel.

Seeing Stanislus kneeling at the altar, the king grabbed him from behind and stabbed him to death.

Mary Khoury
Lebanon 1991

Mary was seventeen years old when Damour, her village in Lebanon, was raided by Muslim fanatics. They were determined to convert everyone to Islam by force. She and her parents were told: "If you do not become Muslims, you will be shot." Her parents refused, and were immediately killed.

Mary knew that Jesus had been given a similar choice: Give up His profession of being the Son of God and the Savior of the world or be crucified. He chose the cross. So she replied, "I was baptized as a Christian and His Word came to me: 'Don't deny your faith.' I will obey Him. Go ahead and shoot."

The Muslim who had just killed her father and mother shot her and left her for dead.

Two days later the Red Cross came into Mary's village. They found her and her family, but Mary was the only one alive. She was paralyzed, as the bullet had severed her spinal cord. Her paralyzed arms were extended and bent at the elbows, much like Jesus' must have been when He was crucified.

At first Mary was depressed, not knowing what she would do. Then the Lord spoke to her, and she knew what she must do with her life. "Everyone has a vocation," she said. "I can never marry or do any physical work. So I will offer my life to the Muslims, like the one who cut my father's throat, stabbed my mother while cursing her, and tried to kill me. My life will be a prayer for them."

Those Muslims have no idea how blessed they are!

William Tyndale
First Translator of the New Testament into English
England 1536

William Tyndale was the first person to translate the New Testament into English - which was the English of his day. He did this so that ordinary people could read the Bible. This sounds reasonable to us, but in Tyndale's day it caused a storm of protest and persecution against him, especially since the books were printed in Germany and smuggled into England.

The reason for the controversy was that for many centuries the Scriptures had been in the hands of the clergy alone. They had no desire for the common people to know what the Bible said. Bibles were in Latin, which was a language ordinary people could not read. To make certain the common people couldn't take them, the large Bibles in the churches were chained to the pulpits.

Tonsall, the bishop of London, came up with a plan to try to keep Tyndale's New Testaments out of England. He would send someone to Tyndale, who was living in Antwerp in the Netherlands (the Netherlands included Belgium at that time). This person would buy all of Tyndale's New Testaments and give them to the bishop to be destroyed. Tonsall found a clothing merchant named Packington who agreed to help him.

"I can do even more than that," Packington told him, "I know most of the Dutch traders and other merchants who buy Tyndale's books and resell them in England. If you will give me the money, I will buy every book from them that has been printed but not yet sold."

Thinking he had God "by the toe," the bishop agreed. "Do your best, Mr. Packington. Get them for me and I will pay whatever they cost and give you a good profit, for I intend to burn them at Paul's Cross Church in London!"

Packington, however, went immediately to see Tyndale and told him the whole plan. They agreed to sell the bishop all the New Testaments he would buy. That way the bishop of London would have some books to destroy, Packington would have the bishop's thanks, and Tyndale would have enough money to print more books.

Months later, when the bishop learned that more New Testaments were showing up in England, he sent for Packington." How can there be so many New Testaments here? You promised me that you would buy them all!"

Packington replied, "I bought all of them that were available, but obviously they have printed more since then. It will probably get no better so long as they have the shipping stamps to ship the books. You had better buy the stamps also if you want to be sure they won't reach England." At that, the bishop realized he had been tricked, and the matter was ended.

Not long afterward a co-worker of Tyndale's named George Constantine traveled to London. He was discovered and arrested. Sir Thomas More, Lord Chancellor of England, questioned him. "We know there are a great many like you helping Tyndale. Where do you get your money? Who is helping you?"

Constantine replied, "I will tell you. It's the bishop of London who helped us. He buys all the New Testaments we can print, at quite a nice profit too. He has been our only help."

"I thought it was him," More said. "I told him his plan would backfire on him."

It wasn't long before Tyndale translated the Old Testament into English. Now the entire Bible was available to ordinary people in a language they could read, and the outcry against Tyndale and his work could be heard all over England. The clergy said that it was heresy, filled with errors and of the devil. Some said it was impossible to translate the Scriptures into English. Others said it wasn't lawful for ordinary people to have the Bible in their own language. Many said it would make all the people heretics. Those who wanted to persuade the politicians said that it would make the people rebel against the king.

To stop Tyndale's work, the English clergy devised a plan to lure him into the hands of sympathetic authorities in the Netherlands. They would arrest him and try him for heresy. To accomplish their plan, they needed someone who could become friendly enough with Tyndale so that Tyndale would trust him and fall into their trap.

They needed a Judas — and a Judas they found. He was Henry Philips, who went to Antwerp and over several weeks time became friends with Tyndale. Then he lured him into the trap. The entire plan went so smoothly that, after Tyndale was imprisoned, the officers who arrested him said they felt sorry for him, because they had seen how simple and trusting he was.

Tyndale was condemned to death for heresy by religious and secular authorities. On October 6, 1536, in the town of Vilvorde in the Netherlands, God's first translator of the New Testament into English was brought to a place of execution. He was tied to a stake, strangled by a hangman to the point of death and burned in fire for doing God's work.

As he met the Lord, Tyndale cried with a loud voice, "Lord! Open the King of England's eyes!"

Dominggus Kenjam
Indonesia 1999

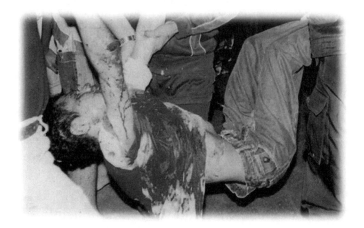

Dominggus Kenjam was a twenty-year-old Bible student at the Doulos Bible School in Jakarta, the capital of Indonesia. He was asleep in his dormitory when he was awakened by shouts of "Allah Ahkbar! Allah Ahkbar! (Allah is God! Allah is God!)." Before he could escape, several Muslims broke into his room, grabbed him, and beat him nearly unconscious with their fists and clubs. Writhing in agony on the floor, Dominggus heard the Muslims say, "We will allow the women to live. The men must die."

Forcing himself to his feet, Dominggus tried to run out of the room, but he was struck across his back and the right side of his neck by the blade of a sickle, nearly cutting off his head. This time he fell unconscious to the floor. Apparently thinking he was dead, his attackers left him lying in a pool of his own blood.

Weeks after his attack, when he had started to mend from his horrendous wound, Dominggus said, "My spirit left my body that night and was carried by angels to heaven. As I went up, I looked behind me and I could see my body lying on the floor. My body wasn't moving, and there was blood all around my head. It was running from an awful cut across the back and side of my neck."

Amazingly, he said, "I did not feel any fear, just a great peace that I had never felt before as I was carried up to my new life in heaven. But when I reached there, Jesus met me and told me that I was to return to earth. He said to me, 'It is not time for you to serve Me here.'"

Back in his body, Dominggus heard the voices of emergency medical workers. They had arrived to take care of the many Bible students who had been attacked. Thinking that Dominggus was dead, they were preparing to take him to the morgue. The problem was, they didn't know whether he was a Christian or a Muslim. They were discussing whether to take his body to a Christian or a Muslim morgue.

Since he did not want to go to any morgue, especially not to a Muslim one, Dominggus prayed to God for enough strength to speak. The strength came, and he hoarsely cried out, "I am a Christian."

Realizing that the student they were preparing to take to a morgue was alive, the medical workers rushed him to the hospital. When the doctors saw how badly Dominggus was wounded, they could hardly believe he was still alive. They also believed that if by some miracle he managed to survive, he would be severely handicapped, mentally and physically.

Dominggus fooled them all, however, and recovered completely. Only the permanent scar around the back and side of his neck remains. Like many who have suffered for Jesus, he has a renewed faith and message of forgiveness. "What the Muslims did to me," he says, "has brought me much closer to God. For the first time in my life I am praying for my Muslim neighbors. I especially pray every day for those who tried to kill me."

Anne Askew

England 1546

Anne was the young, unmarried daughter of Sir William Askew, Knight of Lincolnshire, England. Lincolnshire was the same county in which John Foxe, the author of Foxe's Book of Martyrs, was born in 1516.

Anne was accused of heresy by the secular and religious authorities in England. Her crime was that she refused to believe the things the church taught that were contrary to what she believed the Scriptures taught.

The friends who remained faithful to Anne asked her to write an account of her ordeals. She did, much like Anne Frank kept a diary of her difficult experiences during World War II. Here are some of the things she wrote.

I was examined before the King's Council at Greenwich. During my examination the bishop said to me, "It's the king's pleasure that you turn this matter over to him, and let him decide whether you're a heretic or not."

I replied, "I will not do that. But if it's the king's pleasure to hear what I have to say, then I will show him the truth."

"The king will not listen to your foolishness!"

"If Solomon was considered the wisest king that ever lived, and yet it did not bother him to listen to two common women, how much more should the king hear a simple woman who is his faithful subject."

After more examination about what I said or others said I said, the bishop said, "I will now speak to you as a friend."

I said, "So did Judas when he betrayed Christ."

Then the bishop wanted to speak to me alone. But I refused.

He asked me, "Why do you refuse to speak to me alone?"

"Because the Scripture says that in the mouth of two or three witnesses every matter should stand."

Then the bishop said to me, "You will be burned for your arrogance and heresy!"

I answered, "I have searched all the Scriptures, yet I cannot find that either Christ or His apostles put any creature to death."

"It does not matter," he said, "if you do not recant you will be burned to death!"

"Well, well," I said, "God will see to your threatenings when you stand before Him."

Then I was sent to Newgate Prison. From Newgate I was sent to the Sign of the Crown, where Master Rich and the bishop of London tried to turn me away from God with all the power of their flattering and persuasive words. But I did not for a moment consider eating from the forbidden fruit they offered me.

After that, Nicholas Shaxton came to see me and said, "You should recant as I have done, and all will be well with you as it is with me."

I said to him, "It would have been better for you if you had never been born."

Then they questioned me for a very long time about who the wealthy ladies who were paying for my food and other things I needed in prison.* I told them, "I do not know of any wealthy ladies who have paid for my things. My maid, who has been allowed to visit me, tells of my condition in the streets, and people give her money for me. I know nothing about it beyond that."

They then tried to get me to tell them the names of any ladies or gentlewomen who were of my religious opinions, but I refused to tell them. Because I did not give them the names of anyone, they put me

*In those days, prisoners had to pay for their own food, blankets, and similar items in prison. Otherwise they went without or were given whatever was left over from others and from prisoners who had died or had been executed.

on the rack** and kept me there for a long time. And because I laid still and did not cry out, my Lord Chancellor, the bishop and Master Rich took turns racking me with their own hands until I was nearly dead.

Then the sheriff had me removed from the rack. Involuntarily I fainted, and they immediately revived me. After that I sat on the bare floor for two long hours reasoning with my lord chancellor, who with many flattering words tried to persuade me to give up my opinion. But my Lord God (I thank His everlasting goodness) gave me grace to persevere, and will do so, I hope, to the end.

I was then taken to a house and laid in a bed, with as weary and painful bones as ever had patient Job. I thank my Lord God for the rest. In the midst of my weariness and pain, the Lord Chancellor sent me word that if I would give up my opinion, I would lack nothing I needed, but if I would not I would immediately be sent to Newgate and soon be burned. The serpent tempts the hardest when we are nearest the victory!

I sent the bishop word again that I would rather die than break my faith.

The day of Anne's execution was set, and she was brought into Smithfield, that dreadful place of executions. Being unable to walk because of the torture on the rack, they carried her in a chair. At the stake, they tied her body tightly with a chain to hold her up. There were so many people present that fences were put up to hold them back.

**The rack was a torture device that stretched the body until the bones were out of joint.

Upon the bench at the front of St. Bartholomew's Church were the church and government witnesses — Wriothesley, Chancellor of England, the old Duke of Norfolk, the old Earl of Bedford, the Lord Mayor, and various others. Dry sticks were placed around the feet and legs of those being burned that day. Before they were set on fire, someone on the viewing bench heard that there were bags of gunpowder around the condemned. They became afraid that it might explode and that wood and fire would come flying at the bench. But the Earl of Bedford explained to him that the gunpowder was not laid upon the wood, but around the bodies and necks of the heretics, to end their suffering more quickly.

Then Lord Chancellor Wriothesley offered Anne Askew the king's pardon if she would recant. But she answered in a loud voice, "I have not come to Smithfield to deny my Lord and Master."

And so saintly Anne Askew, enveloped in flames as a blessed sacrifice to God, died in the Lord in 1546. She left a remarkable example of faithfulness for all Christians to follow.

Natalia Gorbanevskaia

Soviet Union 1970

Natalia was a young poet who wrote a book published secretly in the Soviet Union. It appeared in France under the title, *At Noon in Moscow*. In her poems, Natalia wrote of the longing for liberty by the people of the Soviet Union. The book begins with the Scriptures, "I only know that in every city the Holy Spirit warns me that prison and hardships are facing me. However, I consider my life worth nothing to me, if only I may finish the race and complete the task the Lord Jesus has given me—the task of testifying to the gospel of God's grace" (Acts 20:23-24).

Not long after the book was published, Natalia was arrested and put into an insane asylum, because communists believe anyone who loves freedom or Jesus Christ to be insane. There were many such asylums in the Soviet Union at that time, where people went in sane and came out insane. They were not places to make the mentally sick well. They were places to make the mentally well sick.

The asylums were huge buildings that housed thousands of prisoners. There were no walls between the cells, only rows of iron bars. Often one to two hundred prisoners were put into one cell. The floors were made of planks with spaces between them. Day and night you heard every sound: prisoners walking, crying, coughing, sneezing, snoring, raging, cell doors slamming, toilets flushing, thousands of sounds from thousands of prisoners. Often communist police disguised themselves as doctors so they could torture their prisoners by using drugs and medical devices.

There was never silence and never peace — just the sound of madness. Only a strong faith in Jesus could keep the madness out of one's soul. But Natalia went into the asylum sane and came out sane.

Francisco
Peru 1989

Twenty-year-old Bible student Francisco (not his real name) had a burning desire to bring Senderista terrorists to Jesus. He lived in Lima, Peru, a city that had swelled to seven million because of the number of people seeking refuge from murderers in the rural areas.

Francisco did not want to flee. He told his pastor that he wanted to attack, and he was asking God to show him how. God answered His prayer as he was walking past the national palace in Lima one day. A car with an open top raced by, and a man inside launched a mortar shell at the palace. It struck the front of the palace and exploded with devastating fury. Never slowing down, the car disappeared around a corner.

The Peruvian police were immediately on the scene and arrested everyone near the palace. Francisco was among them. He was taken to a maximum-security prison, where he was placed in an exclusive holding area for Senderista terrorists. At that time there were approximately five hundred prisoners there.

Like Paul and Barnabas, Francisco did not waste time grieving over his circumstances. Quietly, gently, he began to preach about Jesus to the terrorists, sharing God's love with them. In the Senderista holding area, twenty-four-year-old Maria listened carefully to what Francisco said.

Maria was a student at San Marcos University in Lima. One of her duties with the Senderistas was to shoot wounded victims through the head to guarantee their death. Could God possibly love and forgive someone like that? He could, of course, and He did. Maria finally found inner peace in Jesus Christ. Her days of killing were over, and her sins were washed away forever.

Francisco was held in prison for a year before his trial. During that time he brought over sixty of the Senderista terrorists to Jesus Christ. When he was finally released from prison, he left behind a new church of Christian believers who regularly met to worship, learn together, and help and encourage each other. Though yet in prison, they were free in Christ. The only one they terrified is the devil!

Lady Jane Grey

England 1554

King Edward VI became king when he was ten years old, but his health was never strong. So the Duke of Northumberland, John Dudley, dominated him and the government of England. When he was just fifteen, Young King Edward contracted tuberculosis. He died in July 1553, just three months before his sixteenth birthday. In the meantime, Dudley had been busy trying to maintain control of England.

Early in 1553, when it became obvious that King Edward was not going to live much longer, Dudley arranged a marriage between Lady Jane Grey and Dudley's son, Guildford. Lady Jane Grey was the daughter of Henry Grey, Duke of Suffolk, and the same age as King Edward. When they were both eleven years old, her father and another nobleman, Lord Seymour, had tried to arrange a marriage between her the young king. The scheme to make her the queen of England had failed, however, and she had returned to her father's home.

Jane was a brilliant student, and under the guidance of her Protestant tutor John Aylmer, who later became bishop of London, she learned several languages. At thirteen she could read and write Greek, and at fifteen she also knew Latin, Italian, French and was learning Hebrew. As a teenager, she married Guildford Dudley, not realizing she was part of his father's scheme to continue to rule England.

John Dudley persuaded King Edward to name Jane as his successor instead of Edward's sister, Mary, who was the rightful heir to the throne and a Roman Catholic. Edward died on July 6, and on July 9 Dudley took Jane before the Privy Council, which was the supreme legislative body at that time. The next day she was proclaimed queen.

The plan fell apart nine days later, however, when the rest of England proclaimed Mary to be queen. Jane and her husband, Guilford, were immediately arrested, imprisoned in the Tower of London and convicted of high treason. Though neither of them had actually committed treason, Queen Mary wanted to keep her royal rival under lock and key.

Unfortunately for Lady Jane and her husband, that winter her father joined an uprising against Queen Mary. This prompted the queen to sign Jane's death warrant in order to prevent any further attempts to make Jane queen. Jane and Guilford were executed on February 12, 1554, seven months after they were arrested.

Guildford was taken out of his cell first and led through the crowd of people. He went out through the bulwark gate (a gate in the fortification walls) accompanied by the sheriff's men and then up Tower Hill to a scaffold, where he was beheaded with an ax. About an hour later, Lady Jane was taken from her cell and led to the central keep (stronghold or jail) within the prison. There, she was also beheaded with an ax.

Lady Jane was widely praised for her beauty and learning. She was obviously not a conspirator, but rather an innocent victim of a political plot to put a Protestant queen on the throne. On the scaffold, she declared she did not want the crown, and she would die "a true Christian woman." She was sixteen years old.

Queen Mary became known as "Bloody Mary." In an effort to return England to the Roman Catholic Church, she revived old laws for punishing heretics. Some three hundred Protestants were burned at the stake, and it is said that she personally ordered over one hundred of the executions.

In 1985, a movie, "Lady Jane," was made of Lady Jane's story. In it, Patrick Stewart, of Star Trek and Captain Picard fame, plays the part of Henry Grey, Duke of Suffolk, and Lady Jane's father.

"Out of the mouths of babes... God has ordained strength."

China 1990

Amelio Crotti had been a prisoner in China and wrote about his experiences. The following is one of his accounts.

From my cell I heard a mother speak soothing words to her child of five, whose name was Siao-Mei. She had been arrested with the child because she had protested against the arrest of her bishop. All the prisoners were indignant at seeing the suffering of the child. Even the prison director said to the mother, "Don't you have pity on your daughter? It is sufficient for you to declare that you give up being a Christian and will not go to church any more. Then you and the child will be free."

In despair the woman agreed and was released. Two weeks later she was forced to shout from a stage before 10,000 people, "I am no longer a Christian." Siao-Mei stood beside her as she denied her faith.

On their return home, little Siao-Mei said, "Mummy, today Jesus is not happy with you."

The mother explained, "You wept in prison. I had to say this out of my love for you."

Siao-Mei replied, "I promise that if we go to jail again for Jesus, I will not weep."

The mother ran to the prison director and told him, "You convinced me to say wrong things for my daughter's sake, but she has more courage than I."

Both went back to prison, but Siao-Mei no longer wept.

John Hooper & the Blind Boy
England 1555

John Hooper was just hours away from his dreadful execution when a blind boy came to the prison and begged to see him. Not long before this, the boy had been imprisoned in Gloucester for confessing the truth of God's Word. He had been cruelly treated in an attempt to make him recant, which he refused to do. Realizing they would never make him do so, and finding some mercy in themselves for his blindness, his jailers let him go. Now the boy insisted on seeing Hooper before the godly man was burned at the stake. When he would not stop asking even when they roughly pushed him away, the prison guards gave in and took him to Hooper's cell.

Inside the cell Hooper questioned the boy about his faith and the reason he had been imprisoned and tortured. "I am a Christian," the boy said, "and I would not believe the things they told that were different than what the Bible said."

Hooper hugged the young blind boy to himself for a moment. Then he held him at arm's length, his hands on his shoulders. With tears running down his checks, he said, "My dear boy, God has taken your outward sight from you for reasons that are known only to Him. But He has given you another sight that is far more precious, for He has given your soul the eyes of knowledge and faith."

Hooper paused for a moment and then put his hands on the boy's matted hair as if blessing him. He said, "God give you the grace to pray continually to Him, my young lad, so that you will never lose that sight, for then you would be blind both in body and in soul."

The next day Hooper was taken to the place of execution. He immediately knelt down to pray since he was not permitted to speak to the many people who had gathered to watch, to encourage and to be encouraged by this great man of God. After he had prayed for a while, a small box was brought and put upon a stool in front of him. "In the box," one of the sheriffs said, "is a pardon from the queen if you will give up your foolish beliefs and renounce your teachings."

When Hooper saw the box and heard those words, he cried, "If you love my soul, do not tempt me with that monstrous thing! If you love my soul, take it away!"

Hooper did not die easily in the flames. He burned for nearly an hour. Yet he was like a lamb, patiently suffering the agony without moving. He was in unbearable agony, and yet with God's grace he died as quietly as a child in bed.

John Hooper reigns as a blessed martyr in heaven, resting in the joys prepared for the faithful in Christ before the foundations of the world. All Christians are bound to praise God and be strengthened by him and others who remained faithful to Jesus in the worst of torments!

A Martyr's Seed
North Korea circa 1998

When the young North Korean man, whom we'll call Kim, walked into his home, his mother could tell that something terrible had happened. His face was streaked with tears, his eyes searched wildly as if trying to see something that was no longer to be seen, and he stuttered so badly that she could not understand him.

After some time he became calm enough to tell her what had happened. "I was with a new friend today, and we were talking and fast becoming best friends. Then two police officers approached us and grabbed him and accused him of being a Christian. One of the officers knocked him to the ground and kicked him several times, and the other took out his gun and said he was going to shoot him.

"But even though he was in pain and the gun was pointed at him, my friend did not get angry or curse at the officers or even look afraid. His face was peaceful, and then he looked directly at me and seemed to smile, as if he was trying to tell me something.

"Somehow I knew what it was. He was telling me that what he believed was the truth, and I should believe what he did. And then the police officer shot him, right in front of me! He killed my new friend for being a Christian.

"Then they threatened me and asked me if I was a Christian. I told them I did not even know what a

Christian was. They said they had better not catch me with one again. I do not understand this at all."

His mother held her head in her hands and wept. Finally she said to her son, "I understand," and began to tell him about Jesus. At times her crying became almost uncontrollable as she felt the pain of never daring to tell her son about Jesus, afraid that something might happen to him like what had happened to his new friend. Yet she praised God that He had not forgotten her son, and that He had brought one of His faithful children to be a witness to him.

She told Kim, "God let you witness the martyrdom of your friend. And as the bullet went into him, a seed of hope went into you."

Early that evening Kim tearfully received Jesus Christ into his heart. A few hours later his three younger brothers came home, and he boldly told them about Jesus. "You should also receive Jesus Christ." Before the evening had passed, that is exactly what they did.

The mother cautiously began to look for Bibles for her new Christian sons, but she could not find any. So Kim secretly crossed the Yalu River into China in search of Bibles. For some time he had no success. Then he met some believers, and one of them showed him a miniature Korean Bible. He pleaded with the believers for some of them, but there were no more available. All the miniature Bibles had already been smuggled into North Korea.

Refusing to accept defeat, Kim said, "I am in need of five thousand of these Bibles. I will be back in one month to pick them up."

When Chinese co-workers of the Voice of the Martyrs heard of Kim's request, they hurriedly printed five thousand copies of the miniature Korean Bible. When Kim returned, he took 2,800 Bibles back into North Korea with him. He would be back for the rest of the Bibles after he distributed the 2,800.

The witness of one young martyr led to the immediate conversion of four souls and gave birth to a new missionary effort in North Korea. Kim and his three brothers are all actively sharing their faith and distributing Bibles, knowing that if they are caught they will suffer the same fate as Kim's friend. But today they are no more afraid of dying in Christ than he was.

A Baby Martyr
China 1970

In August 1970, it was reported that Vladimir, a Christian, was arrested in Shanghai and put in prison. The guards put iron tubes around his legs and tightened them with screws. Then they beat on the tubes with a hammer until the vibrations broke the bones in both legs. They did this to make him confess to imaginary crimes against the Chinese government. But he did not confess, for he had committed no crimes.

Several communist police officers went to his home. A female officer held Vladimir's baby in her hands and told Vladimir's wife, "If you do not sign an accusation against the prisoner, we will smash the head of your child."

Vladimir's wife refused, not believing any human being, especially a woman, would do that to a baby. The woman officer smashed the baby's head against the kitchen wall several times, killing it.

Seeing her baby so brutally murdered, the mother went mad, grabbed a kitchen knife from a table and stabbed the officer. The other police officers shot and killed her. One of the officers kicked her body in anger and said, "She was a fool, a stupid fool! Now she and her baby are both dead, gone forever!"

What these atheists did not know, however, was that the mother and her baby were instantly together again in heaven. For them there is no more hate, no more suffering, no more pain and no more tears. They only experience eternal joy in the presence of God and His Son, Jesus Christ.

A Father and Son
Romania 1975

Florea died in Gherla Prison in Romania. Because he refused to do slave labor on the Lord's day, he was beaten until both arms and legs were paralyzed. The communists would not take him to a hospital to be treated, but left him in his prison cell. There was no running water, no bedding and nothing with which the other prisoners could help him. They had to spoon-feed him, but they did not have a spoon, so they used their fingers.

Florea was the most serene and joyful among them. His face shone. When the other prisoners sat around his bed brooding about their sorrows and complaining that their future outlook was so bad, he would say to them, If the outlook is bad, try the uplook."

After one of the prisoners was released, he went to see Florea's family. He told Florea's nine-year-old son about his father, and that his father had told them he wanted his son to grow up to be a good Christian man.

The boy replied, "I would rather become a sufferer for Christ like my father."

Joshua

Nigeria 2000

Unknown to his Muslim family, Joshua had attended a Christian church. It was there that he was saved and baptized. His father was an Islamic teacher, and when he found out that Joshua had received Jesus, he threatened to kill him and kicked him out of the house. Then other members of his family tried to kill him, so Joshua became a fugitive running for his life.

Where can a thirteen-year-old Nigerian boy run? Where could he go? Who would help? It was too dangerous to stay in the church in which he had been saved. The members of his family who wanted to kill him would find him there. So the church sent him hundreds of miles across Northern Nigeria to a safer Christian city. Unfortunately, some of his irate family members heard about this and followed him. To keep him safe, the underground church passed him along their network to a safe house in yet a different city.

Nevertheless, they couldn't seem to shake Joshua's pursuers, so the church prayed for guidance. While praying, the name of a particular pastor came to mind. He had a special safe house where he discipled converts from the Muslim faith. Joshua went to the pastor's home, which was a small house at the end of a road that was so badly rutted it looked like a frozen seascape. It was there that contacts from The Voice of the Martyrs met Joshua.

"He has been with us for two years, but the school has moved him through five grades," said the pastor. "He catches on quickly."

Because Joshua was a minor, he had to go to a police station and swear that he was staying with the pastor of his own free will because his father had threatened to kill him. A copy of his sworn statement was sent to his father, who had spread the rumor that Christians had kidnapped his son.

Joshua is still attending the school, and the pastor would like to keep him there until he has finished high school. Like many other Christians in Nigeria, Joshua prays not only for the salvation of his family, but also for the salvation of those Muslims who think they win merit from Allah for killing those who have left Islam to become Christians.

Margaret Wilson

Scotland 1685

Margaret Wilson's family were covenanters, those who bound themselves by oath or covenant to maintain Presbyterian worship and doctrine in Scotland. In 1637 King Charles I of England tried to impose Anglican Church rule in Scotland, whose population was predominantly Presbyterian. The Scottish covenanters rebelled. This dispute led to many wars between England and Scotland.

In the Solemn League and Covenant of 1643, the Scots pledged their support to the English parliamentarians in the English Civil War with the hope that Presbyterianism would become the established church in England. This hope was not fulfilled. Then in 1660 King Charles II brought back Anglican rule and denounced the covenants as unlawful. The Scottish covenanters revolted three times — in 1666, 1679 and 1685 — each revolt being more harshly repressed than the previous one. Finally in 1688 the Roman Catholic King James II was overthrown. He was succeeded by Dutch Protestant King William III, who reestablished the Presbyterian Church in Scotland.

However, during the last revolt of the covenanters, Margaret Wilson's family carried on a constant guerrilla warfare against the enemies of the Presbyterian Church. Her father, Gilbert Wilson, was a farmer in Glenvernock. There they hid and cared for covenanter preachers who were being hunted down and executed, and they magnified the Lord at every opportunity.

In February 1685, seventeen-year-old Margaret was hiding with several covenanters from English soldiers who had been pursuing them. After a time they ran out of food. Margaret left their hiding place and traveled through the bitter cold to her home, where she received food and warm clothing. Before she could return, however, she was captured and locked up in the "Thieves' Hole," where they kept the worst kinds of criminals. She was left there for almost two months and then taken to another prison, where she was badgered day and night to change her beliefs. She steadfastly refused.

Margaret's youngest sister, Agnes, had also been caught. She and Margaret were sentenced to be flogged through the streets of Wigtown by the public hangman. They were then to be taken to a designated place and executed. Gilbert Wilson paid one hundred pounds sterling for the release of Agnes, who was absolved of her crime because of her age. But Margaret had to pay for her crime of aiding the covenanters or swear an oath of allegiance to the King of England.

Near Wigtown there was a stream called Bladnoch that was fed by the ocean. It was almost empty when the tide went out and several feet deep when the tide came in. This place was like the Bay of Fundy in Nova Scotia. There, the tides often reach more than fifty feet and rush up small streams so fast that small boats filled with tourists can ride the rushing waters.

On the morning of her execution, while the tide was out, a stake was driven in the bottom of Bladnoch stream and Margaret was tied to it. Along the shore the townspeople gathered, ready to rush in and untie her the instant she relented and swore the oath.

The tide came in and quickly reached Margaret's waist. Her voice rang out, "To You, O Lord, I lift up my soul. O my God, I trust in You; Let me not be ashamed; Let not my enemies triumph over me" (Psalm 25:1-2). Someone had given her a Bible, because her hands and arms were not bound. She opened it and read out loud from the eighth chapter of Paul's epistle to the Romans.

The Spirit itself beareth witness with our spirit, that we are the children of God:

And if children, then heirs; heirs of God, and joint-heirs with Christ; if so be that we suffer with him, that we may be also glorified together.

For I reckon that the sufferings of this present time are not worthy to be compared with the glory which shall be revealed in us.

Romans 8:16-18 KJV

The chapter ends with these words:

Who shall separate us from the love of Christ? shall tribulation, or distress, or persecution, or famine, or nakedness, or peril, or sword?

As it is written, For thy sake we are killed all the day long; we are accounted as sheep for the slaughter.

Nay, in all these things we are more than conquerors through him that loved us.

For I am persuaded, that neither death, nor life, nor angels, nor principalities, nor powers, nor things present, nor things to come,

Nor height, nor depth, nor any other creature, shall be able to separate us from the love of God, which is in Christ Jesus our Lord.

Romans 8: 35-39 KJV

When the water reached Margaret's arms, she tossed the Bible onto the bank of the stream and prayed. Her tormentors, who were now in boats near her, urged her to relent. They reminded her that she was a young girl. If she would just pray for the king and swear allegiance to him, they would release her.

She replied that she would never take the oath, but she would pray for the king's salvation. One of the men pushed her head under water, held it there for some time, and then released it. As Margaret gasped for breath, people on the shore shouted, "Margaret, won't you take the oath?"

Instead she prayed, "Lord, give these men repentance and save their souls."

One of the men cursed at her and said, "We don't want your prayers. Just take the oath."

She replied, "I'll take no sinful oath."

For some reason, the officer in charge ordered her lifted from the stake, apparently thinking that she was going to swear the oath. When the people saw that she was being released, many of the covenanters were heartbroken and cried out, "She has taken the oath!"

Realizing what had happened, Margaret said plainly and loudly so that all could hear, "I will not swear allegiance to an earthly king. I am one of God's children, and I will not take a sinful oath."

At that she was lowered back on the stake and left there as the tide continued rolling in. Soon she could be seen no more — except in heaven, where she was swearing allegiance to and worshiping the only true, eternal King.

Saleema
Pakistan 1999

When teenage Saleema gave her Muslim friend Raheela a Bible, she never dreamed that it would result in her being charged with murder. Not long after receiving the Bible, Raheela received Jesus Christ as her Lord and Savior. When her family heard of it, they demanded that she renounce her conversion and return to Islam. She refused. She also refused to marry the Muslim man her parents had arranged for her to marry. When they tried to force her, she ran away.

Saleema was suspected of helping Raheela escape. So Raheela's family beat Saleema and had her taken to the police station for questioning, along with her pastor. They were both put into prison cells. Her parents were also taken to the station, were beaten by the police and then released.

While confined Saleema was repeatedly beaten, sexually assaulted, and endured other brutal tortures. In the meantime, Raheela's family found her hiding in a government shelter and dragged her home. They again demanded that she renounce her Christian conversion and return to Islam. Again Reheela refused. So her family brought her before the village and had her publicly executed. When this happened, the Muslim authorities charged Saleema with murder. They said that if Saleema had not given Raheela a Bible, then the Muslim girl would not have become an apostate and would not have been executed. If Saleema was found guilty, she would also be executed.

The authorities offered Saleema one way out: denounce her faith in Jesus and become a Muslim. She refused. Again and again she chose to remain faithful. She told her accusers, "I would rather be hung than betray my Lord." While in prison, she sang worship songs to influence her fellow prisoners with the gospel in song.

After some time Saleema was released to wait for her trial but was forced to live in hiding. In Pakistan, Christians who are acquitted in the courts are often murdered in the streets — and no Muslim is ever charged with the crime. The Voice of the Martyrs and other persecuted church organizations publicized Saleema's plight to bring international pressure against the Pakistan authorities. Her case dragged on as Saleema tried to recover physically and emotionally from her mistreatment. She could not attend several of her court appearances because she was physically unable.

On May 6, 1999, the case against Saleema was dropped.

Her desire now is to spend her life sharing the message of God's love. She told members of a VOM team to Pakistan, "If you promise to carry your cross, it will be full of thorns, mountains, and difficulties. But no matter how big the mountain, Jesus will help you overcome!"

Victor Korbel

Czechoslovakia 1975

When eighteen-year-old Victor entered the Czechoslovakian army, he took his Bible and Durer's drawing of "The Praying Hands." When asked why he was taking the drawing, he said, "This will remind me what I should do every day."

The Easter Monday after he entered the army, his parents had an underground church meeting in their home. Suddenly the doorbell rang and two army officers entered. They said, "We brought your son home."

Behind them were four soldiers holding a rough wooden coffin containing Victor's body. His family had not been notified that he was dead, and they were heartbroken. Even so, Victor's sister sat down at the piano and played, "Jesus, lover of my soul." His parents wept over the coffin and said, "Thy will be done."

Later they received a letter from one of Victor's army friends. He wrote:

> We shall never forget the last days we
> spent with him. He used to read to us
> from the Bible, and he spoke about
> God. On Good Friday he asked us to
> go with him to church. We all said
> that we would be glad to, but that we
> needed permission.

"I'll try to get it," said Victor, and he went to our commanding officer.

The officer got mad at him. We could hear him cursing. He accused Victor of poisoning us with religious propaganda. We were not allowed to leave the barracks all that day. Next morning Victor was found dead in the courtyard. He had been shot.

Jeanne Guyon

France 1717

Jeanne Guyon was born in Montargis, France, of Roman Catholic parents. Her full name was Jeanne Marie Bouvier de la Motte. When she was two and a half years old, she was sent to the Ursuline Seminary in Montargis. At four she was placed with the Benedictine nuns, and when she was ten she was sent to a Dominican convent. At the convent she found a Bible that had somehow been left in her room. She spent hours reading it.

When Jeanne was fifteen her family moved to Paris, and she began to move into French society. She was a beautiful young girl and attracted many men, which increased what seemed to be natural vanity.

She married Jacques Guyon when she was just sixteen. He was a wealthy man who happened to be twenty-two years older than she was. Like all young brides Jeanne dreamed of a happy marriage, but hers was far from it. Her husband was sick most of the time, and her mother-in-law hated her and did everything she could to turn her son against his new bride. She had lived with her son before he married Jeanne, and she continued to live with them after their marriage. Her mother-in-law ran the house, giving the servants precedence over young Jeanne and forcing her to perform humiliating tasks.

Nothing Jeanne did was right, no matter how hard she tried. Still, she never complained. She saw it all as God using her afflictions to make her inwardly holy and full of His life. She constantly read Thomas à Kempis book, *Imitation of Christ*, and gave up as many vanities as her young heart would let her.

At twenty she gave up dancing and going to plays and parties. The life of Christ had grown so strong within her that she said to a friend, "I do not know how I could have ever enjoyed those worldly pastimes." Even so, her vanity would not let go of her. Later she often told of how she would spend hours before her mirror tending to her face and hair. She prayed time and again," Oh, God, do something to rid me of this ugly thing, for I cannot get rid of it myself."

Then she got smallpox. When she recovered her beautiful face was covered with pockmarks. Now she had nothing to be vain about, and she rejoiced that she had been set free. Her external beauty decreased, but her inner beauty increased so much that at times she seemed to be caught up into heaven.

When Jeanne was twenty-eight her husband died. He had been sick most of the twelve years of their marriage. Before his death, Jeanne knelt at his bedside and said to him, "I beg your forgiveness for anything I have done that wronged you."

He replied, "I am the one who has done wrong rather than you, my dear wife. I am the one who needs forgiveness. I did not deserve you."

During the years that followed her husband's death, Jeanne moved more and more into the inner life. She increasingly believed that the Christian life did not consist of rules, regulations and rituals, but of the life of Christ in the soul of a human being.

Christianity to her was "Christ in you, the hope of glory" (Colossians 1:27). She wrote to a friend, "When self dies in the soul, God lives. When self is annihilated, God is enthroned."

When she was about thirty-four, Jeanne began to travel and teach the inner life. She traveled throughout France and Switzerland, teaching wherever God led her. During this time she also wrote to many   people, counseling them and leading them gently in the way of the inner life.

As her teachings became more popular and widespread, church authorities began to charge her with heresy because some of her teachings were different than church doctrine. The difference was that the church of her day taught the external life and law, and she taught the internal life and grace. They were bound to clash.

Jeanne had written several books by this time, and many people were reading them. The church authorities began burning them, stealing her mail and harassing her every way they could. In one town a priest gathered every one of her books and burned them in the town square. However, a local merchant bought fifteen hundred copies and distributed them throughout the town after the priest left.

Since nothing stopped the distribution of her teachings or the sales of her books, formal charges of heresy and immorality were brought against her. She was arrested and spent the next seven years in prison. Four of those years were in the infamous Bastille in Paris, France. It was said that in the cell next to her was the man in the iron mask. He was rumored to be the twin brother of Louis XIV, who had imprisoned him in the mask so that he could not oppose Louis and take his kingdom from him.

It was during her second year in prison that Jeanne wrote this short poem: "I ask no more, in good or ill, but union with Thy perfect will." During her last two years in the Bastille, she could not have visitors, speak to anyone or write letters. But a maidservant, who insisted on staying with her throughout her imprisonment, died there.

Later, in writing about her prison experiences, she wrote: "Thou, O my God, increase my love and my patience in proportion to my sufferings. . . . All our happiness, spiritual, temporal and eternal, consists in resigning ourselves to God, leaving it to Him to do in us and with us as He pleases."

During the winter of 1701 Jeanne became ill because of the cold and damp conditions in the Bastille. Louis XIV, knowing he could no longer justify keeping her in prison, released her for six months so that she could recover. He banished her to Blois, one hundred miles southwest of Paris, where her son, Armand Jacques Guyon, lived. Later the king renewed her release for six months more and then indefinitely. Still, she was never really free because she could not leave Blois, and the king could put her back into the Bastille anytime he wished.

Being confined to one city did not stop Jeanne from teaching and helping many to find the peace and joy of the inner life. Thousands traveled to Blois to listen to her teach. She also wrote hundreds of letters as well as her autobiography during that time. Though still a prisoner, she was freer in Christ than those who imprisoned her.

The one who became known throughout the world and generations of Christians as Madame Jeanne Guyon died on June 9, 1717, at the age of sixty-nine. She left behind more than sixty books that have encouraged Christians to seek the deeper, inner life of the heart and spirit in Christ for almost three hundred years.

The truths she wrote about her relationship with Jesus have become spiritual classics and have greatly influenced not only the people of her own time, but such Christians as John Wesley, Hudson Taylor, Jesse Penn-Lewis, Hannah Whithall Smith, the blind song-writer Fanny Crosby, and Watchman Nee. Many leaders of great Christian revivals were touched by this humble woman of God who was persecuted and imprisoned by her government and her church because "she loved Christ too much."

Rosa

Cuba 1998

Here is Rosa's story in her own words.

My name is Rosa. I am a fourteen-year-old student, now in high school. It is a great honor to share my testimony.

I was born in a communist home, where no one could even mention the word God. I remember being a little girl looking at a huge picture of Fidel Castro in our living room.

My parents are atheists. My father used to be a representative of a very important organization called the Communist Youth Union. Now he is in the Cuban Communist Party leadership. My mother is the secretary of the Committee for the Defense of the Revolution. In summary, my home is a communist "nest."

My great-grandmother, however, loves God, and she has been faithful to God through all these years. She used to talk to me about the Lord, and she sowed the seeds of the Lord's Words [in me]. On several occasions I tried to go to church with her, but my parents did not allow me to go.

Years later my parents divorced. Then my mother allowed me to go to church without my father's permission. But later, when I was twelve, my mother tried to get me away from the Lord, organizing and inviting me to go to parties. I went away from the Lord, living in that way. But my great-grandmother persevered in praying for me.

One day I went to church and received the Lord Jesus Christ as my Savior. My life started to change, even my way of dress changed totally. My mother did not accept it then, and neither does she now. She never beat me before, but now she does often.

When my father learned that I was a Christian, he told me to choose God or him. I chose the Lord because I have understood that it is the only thing really worthy for me. I know that God is faithful, and He cares for me and is going to do wonderful things in my family.

My mother got married to a communist man. They have a five-year-old son. They don't allow me to talk to him about the Lord or go to church, but I talk to him secretly about the love of the Lord always. Sometimes, I listen to him praising the Lord.

Now I am studying far away from home. When I first came to this place, I was the only Christian, but I have sown God's Word and now we are four. We meet under a tree, hidden, to share the Word. We feel the presence of the Lord in a special way. We keep sowing and praying that soon we'll be many.

God is faithful. He never forsakes His children. Please pray for me. It is not easy to follow the Lord in a country so hostile to Him, where opposition comes not only from the system but also from our homes. Our parents are blind in this atheistic system and do not understand that we grow and we make our personal decisions.

Mine is Jesus Christ. I will be faithful even at the price of death!

Rosa is very active at church and sings in the girls' choir. Please pray for her continued safety and witness.

Chiu-Chin-Hsiu and Ho-Hsiu-Tzu

China 1977

Chiu-Chin-Hsiu and Ho-Hsiu-Tzu were two teenage Christian girls in Kiangsi, China. They and their pastor were arrested and sentenced to death. As has happened thousands of times in Christian history, the persecutors mocked and scorned them for being so foolish as to die for an unseen God. The officer in charge said to the pastor, who was showing great signs of fear, "If you shoot these foolish young girls, I will let you go home."

He took out his pistol and held it to the side of the pastor's head, as if he was going to shoot him. Trembling with fear and in a quivering voice, the pastor said, "All right. I'll do it."

The young girls waited patiently in their prison cells for the moment of their execution. They comforted each other and prayed quietly together. Soon guards came for them and led them out. A fellow prisoner watched the execution through the barred window of his prison cell. He said that their faces were pale but beautiful beyond belief, infinitely sad but sweet.

They were placed against a wall, and their pastor was brought forward by two guards. They placed him close to and in front of the girls. Then they put a pistol in his hand. The girls whispered to each other, then bowed respectfully to their pastor. One of them said: "Before being shot by you, we wish to thank you very much for what you have meant to us. You baptized us, you taught us the way of eternal life, you gave us holy communion with the same hand in which you now have a gun. May God reward you for all that you have done for us.

"You also taught us that Christians are sometimes weak and commit terrible sins, but they can be forgiven again. When you regret what you are about to do to us, do not despair like Judas, but repent like Peter. God bless you, and remember that our last thought of you was not one of unforgiveness because of your failure. Everyone passes through hours of darkness, and you are passing through yours. We die with gratitude for all you did for us and with sadness for what you are now doing to us."

The girls bowed again to their pastor, closed their eyes and stood silently waiting. They were holding hands and praying softly. They believed that fear for his own life had obviously hardened the pastor's heart toward them and toward Jesus.

The pastor raised the pistol and shot the two young girls who had entrusted their spiritual life to him. No sooner had the girls fallen to the ground dead, than the communist guards pushed the pastor against the wall, stepped quickly back, and shot him. As they did this, no one heard words of repentance, only sounds of crying and screaming.

Paul Modi

Sudan 2000

It was a beautiful Sunday morning in central Sudan, and ten-year-old Paul Modi and his parents and two brothers were on their way to church. They were looking forward to an entire day of worship and fellowship on what looked like an absolutely perfect day. But Sundays in Sudan are especially dangerous for Christians, and the Modi family never made it to church.

As they walked along, talking and laughing together, radical Islamic raiders sprang out of the bushes. Swinging long, razor-sharp knives called "pangas," they first charged Paul's father and then his mother, slicing them into pieces.

The three boys watched in horror as their parents were killed. They were so shocked and filled with fear that they had neither the strength nor courage to run into the bushes and escape. The Islamic radicals grabbed the three frightened boys and carried them, kicking and screaming, into the bush.

Hidden from the road, they built a roaring fire and threw the three screaming boys on top of it, laughing as they watched them twist and burn in the flames. Fighting to get out, the older and younger brothers sank deeper into the fire and burned to death. But Paul somehow managed to roll out of the fire on the far side from their attackers. Hidden by the roaring flames and smoke, he escaped into the bush.

At the time of this writing, Paul Modi is living in a refugee camp in southern Sudan. On the back of his head and hands he carries forever the marks of the fire that took his two brothers from him. In his heart he carries forever the memory of his parents' death at the hands of the Islamic raiders.

Paul is not the only one suffering in the Sudan. Hundreds of thousands have lost family members in the civil war that has spanned almost two decades. There are hundreds of thousands of children who cannot go to school, barely have enough to eat and no longer have parents. They have never known peace in their homeland, and they suffer only because they and their parents are Christians.

Valentina Saveleva
Soviet Union circa 1965

Valentina is a young Russian Baptist who spent five years in jail for her faith. When released, she wrote about the conditions in the prison when she was confined.

We were often knee-deep in the mud. Our coats and boots were never dry. There was no washroom. The water was not drinkable because of the salt in it.

Many of us had to sleep on the dirt floor. There were not enough blankets to keep warm. When we awakened in the morning, we had to be careful not to rise too quickly, for our hair was frozen to the floor.

It was impossible to remain free from lice. Many died of tuberculosis. Food was scarce and hardly edible. The temperature was seldom above 41°F.

The prison was full of demon-possessed criminals who cursed night and day. They wanted to destroy my faith in Christ. But they could not.

Robert Thomas
Korea 1886

Robert was barely into his twenties when he was ordained as a minister in a little church in Hanover, Wales. Just a month later on June 4, 1863, he and his young wife were sent to Shanghai, China, by the London Mission Society. Unused to the harsh life and strange food at a foreign missionary station, his wife fell ill two months after they arrived and died within a few days.

In 1866, after having evangelized for a few months in the southern part of Korea, Thomas traveled on the American ship, General Sherman, up the Taedong river. In a shallow part along the river, the ship was grounded on a sandbar. Korean soldiers on shore, not having seen many vessels of this type, became suspicious and scared. Perhaps they thought there were foreign soldiers on board. Waving long knifes they boarded the General Sherman and started killing the passengers and crew.

When Thomas saw that he was going to be killed, he held out his Korean Bible to them and said in their language, "Jesus, Jesus." A soldier swung his long knife at Thomas and knocked the Bible from his hands. With another swing he cut through Thomas's neck. They threw Thomas's head into the river, followed by his body.

It seemed to many that Thomas's missionary voyage into that dangerous area of Korea was a failure and a waste of a young life. But God does not look at things the way we do, and His ways are not our ways.

Twenty-five years after Thomas's death, an American visitor stayed at a small guesthouse near the area of the river where Thomas was killed. One day he noticed strange wallpaper in the main room. The paper had Korean words and numbers printed on it. He asked the owner of the house, "What is this strange paper you've got on your walls?"

The owner told him how Thomas had been killed on the river just a short distance from there. He said, "I found Robert Thomas's Bible. It had his name in it, and I cut out the pages and used them to cover my walls."

At first the visitor wasn't certain if that was the right thing to do with a dead missionary's Bible. But then the owner said, "I am a Christian, and for twenty-five years many people have come to my house to read Robert Thomas's Bible." He paused for a moment and ran his hand lovingly over the covered wall. With tears in his eyes, he said, "When the people leave here after reading my wall, they don't always remember what they read, but they always remember Robert Thomas and how he gave his life serving Jesus Christ."

Johannes Mantahari
Indonesia 1999

Eighteen-year-old Johannes was living in a small village on Halmahera Island. At three in the morning he was awakened by a villager who was shaking his arm. He was told that a large mob of Laskar jihad troops had gathered nearby and was headed for the village looking for Christians.

Johannes dressed quickly and attempted to get out of the village before they arrived, but he was too late and was caught by about twenty radical Muslim warriors. He tried to fight them off, but five of them pinned him to the ground. The others surrounded him so he could not escape and threatened him with a samurai sword.

One of them asked Johannes, "Do you want to become a Muslim?"

He replied, "No."

"We will kill you if you refuse."

"I am prepared to die," Johannes said, fully expecting he would.

One of the Laskar jihad troops struck Johannes on the left temple and then sliced into his left shoulder and forearm with the razor-sharp tip of a samurai sword. Another Muslim took the sword and cut a gaping crevice into the back of Johannes's neck, barely missing his spinal cord.

As he lay face down on the ground, bleeding heavily from the wounds, they swung the samurai sword back and forth across his back and legs, making more gaping wounds. To finish off their gruesome work, they covered Johannes with banana leaves and tried to set them on fire to burn his body. But the leaves were too green and wouldn't burn. After trying several times, the Muslim warriors gave up and left.

Johannes lay on the ground bleeding heavily as the Laskar jihad troops fled into the jungle. With what he was certain were his last few breaths of life, he cried out to God for help. Suddenly he felt enough strength in his arms and legs to throw off the banana leaves, stagger to his feet, and run into the shelter of the jungle. Near dawn, he found a cave and crawled inside.

As Johannes waited in the dark until he was certain he could leave safely, his wounds stopped bleeding heavily. After he left the cave, he staggered blindly through the jungle for eight days trying to find help. He found no one.

Finally, he could go no farther and collapsed on the ground, certain for the second time that he was about to take his last breath. Again he cried out to God. It was night and there was no moon. He couldn't see anything, and he was surrounded by the sounds of the jungle. Then he felt a comforting hand circle his arm and touch his hand. He could not see anyone, but it was a peaceful, reassuring touch. He shouted, "Who is it? And how did you get here in the middle of the night when no one has been in sight?" There was no answer.

The hand withdrew from his arm, but before it did Johannes felt a warm surge of energy go through his body. He now had enough strength to go on. Not long after that his brother-in-law, who had been searching for him, found him in the jungle. He cleansed his wounds and took care of him until he regained his strength. Johannes believes his comforting visitor was Jesus, because in his eight-day search for help in the jungle he had found no one, only countless corpses.

Today Johannes is studying to be an evangelist. He believes that the Lord spared his life so that he could lead many Muslims to Jesus. He sees his multiple scars as badges of honor for the Lord, and he forgave his attackers as "our Father in heaven forgave us."

Sophie Botcharova and the Young People

Soviet Union 1990

Sophie and several other young people were converted in the underground Baptist Church of Elektrostal in Russia. The local communist authorities left this church alone when it had only elderly people in it, but when the young people joined it, they began persecuting it. Wherever the Sunday church meeting was held, the police would show up, break up the service and arrest the leaders. The leaders were always given large fines, far larger than they could pay. So every time they were arrested the members of the church had to collect money to pay the fines for them.

Because the church had not been persecuted before the young people joined it, some of the elderly sisters became frightened and began to resent the presence of the young people. At the same time, the young people began to realize that they were a burden to the church.

The leaders of the church held a special meeting. They asked for volunteers who were committed enough to Jesus Christ to work in an underground printing facility. Sophie and most of her friends joyfully accepted. Several of the older Christians, however, and even some of the young people, refused to help. They said they did not have the necessary skills.

Hearing this excuse, Sophie asked one of the leaders, "Could I say something?"

"Oh course," the leader said.

Sophie stood up and looked around the room and said, "I cannot accept this as a reason to refuse. Nobody can have fewer abilities than I. God does not seek talent, but souls ready for sacrifice. He gives the abilities. I have already experienced this in my life."

The working conditions at the printing facility were difficult and oppressive. There was only one small room, and in that room they had to make space for the printing press, large quantities of paper, a kitchen, and a place for eight people to sleep. Each group of eight stayed at the facility for several days at a time, sometimes weeks, so that the police would not see them traveling back and forth to their homes.

There was only one window in the room, which was darkened and heavily boarded so that no one could look into the room or enter through the window. As a result, there was never any sunlight, very little fresh air, and no way anyone could get a normal amount of rest. However, even under these difficult conditions the small underground printing facility produced over 500,000 pieces of Christian literature — right up to the day communist rule crumbled and it could finally unboard the window and let the air and sunlight in.

Sophie worked at the printing facility more often, harder and longer than anyone else. She was always cheerful and full of joy, as if she was working on a hilltop in the bright sunlight and fresh air, surrounded by trees and flowers and all of God's glorious creation. But she never got to enjoy those

130

things on earth, for after twelve years of working and living in the drab, airless room, she died of lung cancer.

Sounds tragic, doesn't it? But hear Sophie's last words: "The world does not exist for me anymore. Gardens bloom around me. I am raptured by this supernatural beauty. I wait for my Lord."

Dietrich Bonhoeffer

Germany 1945

When only fourteen years old Dietrich Bonhoefer felt called to be a minister and theologian, much to the disappointment of the other members of the wealthy Bonhoeffer family. His family tried to change his mind by criticizing the church, but young Dietrich told them, "I will reform it." And he did.

At the age of twenty-one he completed his theological studies at the University of Berlin. The thesis he wrote as part of his studies was titled, "The Communion of Saints." It was praised as a theological miracle by his professors and others.

All though his life as an ordained minister, theology professor and author, Dietrich probed the heart of religious questions and issues. When he saw that the church in Germany had strayed from its path, seeking the comfort of the world rather than seeking the lost, he spoke out against it.

In 1933 Hitler became chancellor of Germany. As he rose in power, the church in Germany adopted the "Aryan Clause," which denied the pulpit to ordained Jewish ministers. Dietrich openly opposed the action as immoral. He formed the "Pastor's Emergency League," pledging to get the Aryan Clause repealed —while the majority of the church leadership said nothing.

Dietrich traveled to America in 1939 for a one-year speaking tour, but he returned to Germany after only five weeks. He said that he knew he would not have the right to participate in rebuilding Christian life in Germany if he did not share in the trials his people were facing.

During the war Dietrich constantly resisted the evil actions of the Nazis. Through lectures and published articles, he rebuked the church for not having "raised its voice on behalf of the victims and . . . found ways to hasten to their aid." Because of his opposition to Hitler and the Nazi Party, he was arrested on April 5, 1943, and placed in Tegel Prison in Berlin. He was charged with "subversion of the armed forces." He continued to write while in prison.

In 1945 Dietrich was moved to the Flossenbürg Concentration Camp. He was hanged with six other resisters on April 9 — just three weeks before Hitler committed suicide. The camp doctor watched Dietrich kneel and pray before being led to the gallows. Later, he said that he had "hardly ever seen a man die so entirely submissive to the will of God."

In his writings, Dietrich reproved the church: "The church was silent when it should have cried out." His life and his death are a testimony to us. His passion for righteousness in the body of Christ is permanently engraved on paper. You can read it in such books as *The Cost of Discipleship*, and *Letters and Papers from Prison*.

Yun

China circa 1990

When he was sixteen, Yun was told that there was a book called the Bible that tells the way to heaven, and that there was a man who lived about thirty-five miles away who had one. Not having any means of transportation, Yun walked all the way and found the man with the Bible. After he had spent some time there, the man became so impressed with Yun that he gave him the priceless book.

Not long after Yun met an older, uneducated Christian, and together they began telling about Jesus from village to village. This soon caught the attention of the communist police. They started watching Yun and his companion closely. Whenever they appeared in a village, the police tried to catch them talking about Jesus or to catch Yun reading to the people from the Bible.

Yun had read in 1 Samuel 23:13 that David pretended to be crazy to escape from his enemies. So whenever the police came around, Yun would do the same thing. He did it so well that the police would do nothing but laugh at him and let him go. When they left, Yun would get serious again and speak to the people about Jesus and salvation.

Eventually, however, the police caught on to what Yun was doing. They arrested him and put him in prison, where he was beaten several times in an attempt to make him confess to certain crimes against the government. When he refused, he was tried publicly in a village marketplace.

Yun was small and thin. He had no shoes, and his clothes weren't much better than rags. His body was covered with bruises, and his face was deformed from all the beatings. The communist judge said to him, "We will give you one last chance to save your life. If you leave this illegal underground church and join the "Three-Self Patriotic Church" (which collaborates with the communist government), we will give you fine clothes and make you one of its leaders."

Yun did not answer. He was silent before the judge, just as Jesus was silent before Herod. This enraged the judge, and he had a doctor brought to the marketplace to make Yun speak. The doctor told him, "I will heal your dumbness," and forced needles under his fingernails.

Yun passed out from the pain and fell to the ground. Every time he started to come to, the policemen walked on his body, saying, "Your stubbornness led to this." When he still refused to speak, he was taken back to prison, where the other prisoners were forced to urinate on him.

Yun's only treasure in prison was a tin cup on which he had managed to paint a cross. One day one of the guards threw it into the common toilet, and Yun fished it out. He clutched it to his chest, tears running down his cheeks.

Yun was kept in prison for ten years for his crime of speaking to others about Jesus and refusing to join the Three-Self Patriotic Church. During that time, he fasted often and prayed for the Chinese underground churches and his fellow prisoners. When released, he was still strong in his faith. He continued to refuse to compromise with the world or with any church that was controlled by the communist government.

Richard Okill

South Africa 1993

At St. James Church in South Africa, black gunmen of the Pan African Congress ran into the sanctuary and down the aisles, firing at the church members with automatic weapons, rifles and pistols. They killed ten members and wounded dozens of others.

Seventeen-year-old Richard Okill, whose father is a pastor, was sitting in a pew next to two girls when the gunmen started firing. He yelled at the girls, "Get down on the floor," and then threw himself on top of them to protect them. He was shot in the back several times, but none of the bullets struck the girls he was protecting. He died so they might live.

After the attack, over one thousand supporters of PAC marched past the church chanting, "One settler — one bullet!" and "One church — one bomb!" They demanded that "all missionaries be expelled from the country."

Since the time of Jesus' crucifixion and resurrection, His enemies have tried to destroy His Church. But they have never been able to because His Church is made up of saints like Richard Okill, who are willing to die for the sake of others—just like their Lord did.

Graham, Philip and Timothy Staines

India 1999

Graham and Gladys Staines lived in an old house at the Mayurbhanj Leprosy Mission in Mayurbhanj, India, with their three children, Esther (fourteen), Philip (eleven) and Timothy (seven). They were Australian missionaries who worked in the treatment center there.

In January 1999 Graham took Philip and Timothy with him on his annual trip to a leprosy hospital in Manoharpur, a tiny village nestled in the remote hills of Keonjhar, about 155 miles north of the Orissa state capital. Orissa had the highest incidences of attacks against Christian churches in India—some sixty attacks between 1986 and 1998. Graham was aware of this, and he also knew that some of the tension had found its way to Manoharpur, But he wasn't worried. He and his wife and children had decided a long time before to follow Jesus wherever He led them to minister to lepers, and Manoharpur was one of those places.

There was no electricity, running water or modern conveniences in the village of Manoharpur. Philip and Timothy and their father slept in the back of their station wagon. It had more than enough room for them and comfortable bedding, which they carried on trips to these remote areas.

The boys always enjoyed traveling with their father, and he enjoyed having them along. They had already developed a love for these simple people and the lepers that their parents treated. Graham hoped that someday they would follow in his footsteps and join him in this work to which he and his wife had devoted their lives. The boys gave all the indications of intending to do so.

India was their home now, and it always would be. They loved the people and could not imagine living and working anywhere else. God had brought them here, and God poured His love through them as they ministered to the lepers and treated their sores. One former leper, a young woman named Sarida, said about the Staines:

Our world was darkness. We always faced death. None of the religious leaders bothered to give us even one meal. When we begged for alms, they would throw stones at us and chase us away. We were untouchables.

These religious leaders used to tell us that we deserved leprosy because of our sins in our previous birth—because of our karma. And we were left to die in the jungles all alone, like worms.

But then came Staines Dada and his daughter and sons. They stretched forth their hands of mercy to us and to the Leprosy Home. There we saw the love of God.

Dada and his wife would personally wash our sores and dress the wounds with medicines. And when we were cured, they would teach us some skills and give jobs to us. . . . Philip and Timothy, what loving kids, they used to come and play with us lepers, the outcasts of society.

Sarida was overcome with grief and unable to speak any longer.

On the night of January 22nd in Manoharpur, Graham fixed the bed in their station wagon, and they all climbed in to settle down for the night. It had been a hard day, and they were all tired. Philip and Timothy were more tired from play than from work. They had been running around the village playing with the other children, though they were always willing to help their father when he needed them.

Before they went to sleep, they did what they always did on these trips. They talked about Jesus for a while, and then each said a prayer. Graham loved to hear his boys pray, especially seven-year-old Timothy, who still prayed in the innocence and simplicity of a young child.

About three hundred yards from their station wagon, a group of young men were playing drums and enjoying a traditional Indian dance. The rhythmic beat of the drums helped the two boys and their father fall asleep quickly and soundly. Tomorrow was going to be another busy day.

But there wouldn't be any tomorrow for them.

At about eleven o'clock on January 22nd, a group of radical Hindus led by a man named Dara Singh left Jamadwar and headed for Manoharpur. Singh was no stranger to the police, having been arrested several times for inciting violence. Singh and his mob arrived at Manoharpur about 12:20 a.m. on January 23. They came in through the fields, armed with axes and tridents (three-pronged spears). They had just one target: the Staines station wagon where Philip and Timothy and their father slept.

As the terrorists came near the vehicle, they started screaming as loud as they could, like wild animals that had gone mad. Singh struck first, swinging his axe at the tires and slashing them so the vehicle could not move. The others broke the windows and began striking the Staines, beating all three unmercifully with their fists and clubs. Graham tried to shelter Philip and Timothy with his body. He was beaten savagely until he could no longer protect them.

After beating all three nearly unconscious, the raging mob then repeatedly stabbed them, thrusting their tridents through the broken windows again and again in a wild frenzy. Singh piled straw under the vehicle and set it on fire. In seconds, the station wagon was engulfed in flames. Through the broken windows Graham could be seen holding Philip and Timothy close to him. Anyone who knew him was certain that the one word he would be speaking to them over and over was "Jesus."

Someone ran up with a bucket of water to try to douse the flames, but they were chased away by the murderers who circled the vehicle, shouting and laughing as Philip and Timothy and their father were roasted alive.

Dr. Subhankar Ghosh, a close friend of Graham's, remembers vividly every moment of that terrible night.

We had dinner with the Staines around 9 p.m., and they went to sleep in their station wagon, parked near the church, at about 9:45. I was sleeping in one of the huts, only about three hundred feet from the church.

[Just after] midnight, we were woken up by some strange shouts and screams, and I peeped through the side window. I couldn't believe what I saw. I heard shouts, screams, beatings, breaking of doors. There were fifty to sixty people with burning torches in their hands . . . shouting "beat, beat" around the station wagon.

Soon they started smashing the windows of the jeep with bars and sticks. The frenzied mob blocked Graham from escaping with Philip and Timothy. They were brutally beaten.

Then suddenly I saw the jeep in flames. I knew my dear friends would be burned into ashes. The attackers had already blocked the doors of the village huts so that no one could get out and help the Staines. A few who did get out and questioned the mob were threatened [with beatings and burning themselves].

The villagers said the attackers were shouting "Victory, Dara Singh." The attackers also burned another jeep, parked nearby, and its driver was beaten and chased away. After an hour, the furious militants fled the scene.

[We freed our doors and raced outside.] We could not believe what we saw. We were numbed. Graham was an embodiment of Christian love and compassion. And Philip and Timothy—tender, cheerful, who used to play with the lepers and their children! Is there no limit to man's wickedness?

Hasda, the driver of the station wagon and a co-worker with the Staines for over twenty years, gave his report of the burning.

I was woken up by the screams of some people. There were about fifty to sixty men around the jeep where Saibo and children were sleeping. They were smashing the vehicle with staves and stones. Some carried tridents also. Then I saw somebody putting a bundle of straw under the vehicle and setting it on fire. I brought water and tried to put out the fire, but some of them caught me and beat me hard and chased me away.

I ran to Murmu's hut and informed him, and he ran to call the village chief. When I returned to the vehicle, what I saw was most tragic. Fire had devoured the two vehicles, and my Saibo and little Philip and Tim [were] turned into ashes.

I am sorry I couldn't do anything to save my Saibo and the little ones. My parents were cured lepers and inhabitants of Rajabasa rehabilitation center. I was born there. The Staines treated me like their son. Philip and Tim used to play with my children [and] take them on their cycles. The future of the mission is [now] in God's hands. Our Lord is able.

Gilbert Venz, a friend of the Staines from Australia who had accompanied Graham and his two sons to the village, was also at Manoharpur that night. He painfully relates, "The village had turned in for the night, but at about 12:30 midnight, what seemed like a large group of men began raising a commotion in the street outside. They were screaming, 'Don't come out! We will kill you!' I was indoors and we found that the door had been blocked from outside. Graham and the kids were sleeping in the jeep."

Because he was trapped inside, Venz didn't know the station wagon had been set on fire. He heard the terrifying noise of the mob, and when the shouting subsided someone freed his door. He rushed out, ran toward the station wagon and found only a burned out, smoking shell—and three bodies. They were charred beyond recognition but locked in a tight embrace. In life and in the agony of their deaths, Graham and his sons had been inseparable.

A number of people who fled the raging mob said that they saw a wide beam of bright light shining down on the burning station wagon. "I do believe," said Gladys Staines, "that my husband and children were specially strengthened by my Lord and the angelic hosts from heaven." Asked if she would leave India and their work with the lepers, she replied, "Never. My husband and our children have sacrificed their lives for this nation. India is my home. I am happy to be here. I hope to die here and be buried along with them."

Ivan Belousov and the Monks
Soviet Union 1982

In October 1982, a seventeen-year-old Pentecostal named Ivan Belousov was tortured with a blowtorch until his body was burned so badly that he died. This happened on the seacoast near Nakhodka, a small town fifty-five miles southeast of Vladivostok. His torturers were never found.

The KGB warned Ivan's father that if the incident became known outside of the Soviet Union, a rumor would be spread that Ivan was burned to death by Christian believers. The Pentecostals made it known anyway and included an appeal to all Christians to, "pray for us because we are all the body of Christ, and if one limb hurts, so does the whole body." They signed the appeal, "Wives, mothers and children whose husbands, sons and fathers are in prison."

About the same time as Ivan Belousov's torturous death, a small commune of Orthodox monks was scattered outside the city of Suihumi. Eighteen of them sought shelter in a cave. Communist authorities pursued them in a helicopter. When they found where they were hiding, they lowered a barrel of flammable liquid to the cave exit and ignited it. All the monks inside the cave burned to death.

Captain X and the Twelve-Year-Old Boy

Romania 1974

In a 1974 VOM newsletter, Pastor Richard Wurmbrand, founder of The Voice of the Martyrs, wrote about a man he called Captain X and a twelve-year-old boy.

One day the guards pushed a new prisoner into a cell where only Christians were detained. He was shorn [hair clipped short], dirty and thin. At first nobody recognized him. But after a few minutes one exclaimed, "This is Captain X!"

He was one of the worst torturers of Christians. He had arrested and beaten many of those with whom he now shared the prison cell. They surrounded him and asked how he had come to be in prison. With tears rolling down his checks, he told his story.

A couple of months before, while sitting in his office, a boy of twelve entered, holding in his hand a flower for the captain's wife. The boy told him, "Captain, you are the one who put my father and mother in prison. Today is my mother's birthday. I always buy her a flower on this day. Because of you I have no mother to gladden today, but she is a Christian and taught me to love my enemies and reward evil with good. So I thought I would bring a flower to the mother of your children. Please, take it to your wife and tell her about my love and about the love of Christ."

It was too much even for the communist captain —he embraced the child. He could not torture any more, nor keep his position. He considered it a privilege to sit now in prison with those whom he had imprisoned before.

Forgiving love is the key of victorious Christian life.

Addil

Sudan 2000

Ten-year-old Addil and most of his young classmates have to walk an hour from their homes in the village of Kauda, Sudan, to attend classes at Holy Cross School. For most Westerners this is a tough journey, even with expensive walking shoes. But Addil makes his way along the stone-covered path with little difficulty. The soles of his bare feet are like leather from walking long distances through the Nuba Mountains where he lives. In that region there are no roads or cars, and while a few families are fortunate enough to own a camel or donkey, Addil has only his legs for transportation.

One hot Tuesday morning in late February, Addil's teacher moved the English class outdoors because there was a cool breeze blowing. Most of the children were ten or eleven years old. They were sitting in little groups writing the English assignment their teacher had given them when they heard the sound of an airplane engine. Because planes often passed overhead, they recognized the engine sound as that of their government's Antonov cargo planes. After glancing up for a moment, the students went back to their work.

This morning the government plane was carrying something more than its usual cargo. It was carrying four bombs for the Holy Cross School. As the plane passed directly overhead, the side door opened and the bombs were dropped on the students below.

All but one of the four bombs exploded, throwing hot shrapnel in every direction. It tore through the bodies of the young children and their teacher, killing many instantly, mortally wounding several, and wounding and maiming others. In the end twenty-two people died, mostly the students and their teacher.

Addil was one of the students who was maimed. When the bombs exploded, shrapnel tore through his left arm, tearing flesh and muscle to shreds and mangling his arm so badly that it had to be amputated at the elbow.

Although Addil still walks up the stone-covered path from his village to Holy Cross School, the headmaster of the school says that the attack has changed his personality. He used to be a happy, carefree young boy, full of life and fun. Now he is withdrawn, quiet and seldom laughs. Like many of his classmates who survived the vicious attack, he no longer runs and plays in the school yard.

In 1 Corinthians 12:26, the apostle Paul says that if one member of the body of Christ suffers, all the members suffer with them. When Addil lost his left arm because of his government's persecution of Christians, we all lost a bit of ourselves.

Alexander Sazepa
Soviet Union 1944

The underground church in Russia reported that this poem was written by a young Russian soldier, Alexander Sazepa. It was found in his coat after he died in battle in 1944 and then translated into English.

Hear me, O God, I never spoke with you before.
Today I tell you the first time, "Welcome!"
Since we were children they brainwashed us:
"There is no God!"
And I, like an idiot, believed it.

I never mused about your creation.
Today it is as if I could see for the first time
The stars from my hole made by a grenade.
Here I understood suddenly how terrible a
deception can be.

I speak to You, though not knowing if you will
give me a hand.
You'll understand me.
How strange that Your light appeared to me in
this hell, And that I can experience You.
I'll tell you this one thing, that I am joyous to
have known You.

At midnight they will sound for attack, but
I don't fear.
Your look will rest on us.
Hear the signal! I go. I felt so well with You.
Just one more word: You know the battle
will be fierce.
Maybe I'll knock at Your gate tonight.

Though I was not Your friend, will You allow
me to enter?
I weep and, lo, my eyes open.
Goodbye, my God.
I go and probably will not return.
How strange! I look death in the eyes
without any fear.

Safeena

Pakistan 2001

For teenage Safeena, her only crime in the Muslim nation of Pakistan was being a Christian. It was a crime that put scars on her body and her mind, but she willingly carries them to honor the name of her Lord and Savior, Jesus Christ.

As a teenage Christian in Pakistan, Safeena's opportunities for education and employment are highly limited. In 2000 she worked as a household helper for a wealthy Muslim family, cooking and cleaning to earn money to help support her family. Because Safeena is an attractive young girl with dark brown eyes and a quick, warm smile, one of the sons in the Muslim family found her highly desirable and decided that he wanted to marry her. The problem, however, was that she was not a Muslim.

As always happens in Muslim countries in this kind of situation, Safeena's employers began to pressure her to renounce her faith in Jesus and turn to Islam, so she could marry their son and become part of their family. But Safeena refused, telling them again and again, "I am a Christian." As the pressure increased Safeena wanted to leave, but her family's poverty forced her to keep the job for the meager income it provided.

Finally the young man gave up on having Safeena for his wife and decided to take her by force. One day while she was working in the home, he dragged her into a room and sexually assaulted her. Shattered in every way possible, Safeena quit her job and refused to go back to the home where her attacker lived. Before Safeena and her family could bring charges against the son, the Muslim family accused her of stealing from them. Safeena was immediately arrested and locked up at the local police station.

Sitting in the jail cell, it did not seem to Safeena that things could get any worse, but they soon did. The young man who had sexually assaulted her came to the jail and was allowed to enter her cell, where he assaulted her again. Then the police officer who was assigned to guard her also assaulted her.

There are no words to describe how Safeena felt.

As of this writing Safeena is released on bail but still faces charges of stealing from the Muslim family. Her life is forever changed. She has little prospect of ever finding a husband, for in Pakistan women who are sexually assaulted are considered shameful. Her family may have to move to another part of Pakistan for her safety and theirs.

In spite of all these devastating experiences, Safeena's faith in Jesus Christ remains strong. She knows that while her earthly home is fearful and uncertain, her heavenly home is safe and secure. Still, she needs the prayers of all her Christian brothers and sisters, especially the young who can understand what it is like for her to endure terrible things. We must pray for Safeena's emotional and physical healing and that her future will be safer and brighter than her past.

Spartak Tagayev
Tajikistan circa 1998

Twenty-one-year-old Spartak Tagayev, a Tajik Christian, was blinded by a bomb that was planted in his church by fanatical Muslims. When workers from The Voice of the Martyrs came to help him and his church, he told them, "The main thing is to look to God and always trust Him, whatever happens. Earlier, when all this happened, I could not say thanks to God, but in a while I understood.

"Now I tell everyone. 'It is not only that I am all right, I am perfect!' Nothing oppresses my spirit, and I do not fall into depression or despondency. Whatever happens, one should trust Jesus always and in all circumstances. Sometimes it is very difficult to do so, especially when one cannot understand a lot of things. Now, that is where one should always display special trust in Jesus.

"As long as we are on this earth and in this body, we will have sorrow. Sufferings and trails will not last long. We will all face God, and He will make up for everything that we lost here on earth. We should be strong!

"I am studying how to play a guitar, and I want to become a missionary in future, of course, if it will be God's will. I wish to tell all nonbelievers, 'Believe in Jesus Christ, because Jesus Christ is salvation, the door to the kingdom of heaven.'"

Heroic Christian Children
Soviet Union 1969

When their Christian parents die in prison, Christian children are often left alone to take care of themselves unless they have Christian relatives or friends who will take care of them. They must find shelter and food where and when they can, even from garbage cans. Or they can give up their Christian beliefs, become atheists and be cared for by the state. But most of these children have learned from their fathers and mothers a sure and certain faith.

Surprisingly, in July 1969 the Moscow atheistic magazine, "Nauka i Religia," had an article about Russia's heroic Christian children. The author of the article wrote:

In Kislovodsk I spoke after a religious service with a girl of eleven. She was sincerely convinced that while she prays, the good Lord looks at her and smiles. She said, "There is a God. I see Him in myself. I believe nobody who says that He doesn't exist."

Another little girl kissed an image with Jesus crucified. Then she made her doll kiss it too. When asked why, she said, "God looked at the doll. I saw it."

Who is to say that God is not interested in a little Christian girl's doll?

The magazine article continues with a story about Lurii, a boy of twelve, who said, "In my prayers, I ask God to give me strength to fight those who are against God. We have to fight them not with a sword, but with the Bible."

Another twelve-year-old boy was quoted as saying, "I ask God to forgive my sins, to make me strong, and that there should be no evil in me."

Munira

Tajikistan 2002

Here is Munira's story in her own words.

Although there is freedom in Tajikistan, there is opposition from local Muslims. The spread of Islam is supported by Iranian propaganda and Afghani soldiers. The Tajiks who embrace Christianity experience the fiercest opposition from their families.

That's what I experienced when I was nineteen-years-old and received Jesus Christ as my Savior. At first I felt an overwhelming peace and an immediate release from the bondage I had known trying to follow rules and duties of growing up in a strict Muslim family. After awhile the gravity of my decision hit me. I knew my family would not understand why I had turned away from Islam. I kept my faith private for six months by reading my Bible in secret and slipping away on Sundays to attend an underground church service.

When my family announced that I had to be married in an arranged wedding, I proclaimed my faith in Christ. My grandfather immediately started to beat me. He stopped beating [me] after fifteen minutes only because he had an asthma attack. The beatings continued the next day by my father, a former soldier who had fought in Afghanistan. He locked me in my room saying, "You will never leave until you repent!"

Over the next six months, mullahs [religious teachers] from the mosque visited me, praying and pressuring me to return to Islam, but I resisted. My father reached the breaking point and told me, "Munira, you have five minutes before I kill you. Who do you choose? Your family or Jesus?"

I was so tired and so broken. I was down to my last ounce of faith. I said, "Jesus, my Savior."

For the next two hours my father, whom I loved so much, beat me. All I could do was sob and endure the strikes, all the time wondering how my family could hate me so much. My father then pushed me into our car. He threw a shawl into the back seat and announced that he was going to bury me alive. The only thing that stopped him was realizing that there were still two days left of Ramadan, the Islamic holy month in which Muslims are not allowed to sin.

The next day I happened to hear the phone ring, and I picked it up. The caller, a Christian friend, whispered, "Munira, I will be waiting at the bus stop tomorrow. Meet me there." Despite the terrible beatings, I did not want to leave my family. I loved them and wanted them to accept me and eventually accept Jesus.

During the three weeks away from my family, Jesus' faithfulness was revealed so much to me. After much prayer I knew that the time had come to reconcile with my beloved family.

When I returned home, everyone rejoiced. Everyone, that is, except my father. His first words to me were, "I hate you. My daughter died three months ago. Get out."

I fell at his feet, crying as I hugged his legs. "My God told me to come back. I will never leave you. You can beat me and kill me, but I will stay with you." My father broke down and hugged me.

For the next nine months an uneasy truce existed. My family accepted my Christianity as long as I kept it private. I began working for a Christian organization whose leaders encouraged me to go to a Bible college in the United States. I was excited for the opportunity but desired my father's blessing. When I asked him I covered my eyes, not wanting to see his reaction. Surprisingly he calmly asked, "Are you sure you want to follow this way?"

When I said, "Yes," he responded, "You do what you think is right."

Now that I have devoted myself to Bible classes and to learning more about Christ, I am hoping to return to Central Asia soon to minister to my Muslim brothers and sisters and share Christ's love with them!

Willing to Bleed
Philippines 1997

The small, ten-year-old Filipino girl stood outside the village Christian church listening and watching through the open door. She smiled at almost everything she saw and heard, and sometimes she moved her feet and swayed in time with the worship music. Seeing her, the American missionary went outside and said, "Would you like to come in and join us?"

The girl backed away slightly and said, "Thank you. I would like to, but my father told me to stay away from Christians."

"Why is that?" the missionary asked. "Do we look like bad people or sing bad songs?"

"Oh, no," the girl said." Everybody looks so happy, and I like the music very much. But my father hates Christians and told me to stay away from them." With that she left, often turning around to look back at the church and wave to the missionary.

From that moment on the missionary prayed for the small girl. He prayed for the day when her hunger would be greater than her fear, when she would come into the church and learn about Jesus and receive Him as her Lord and Savior. From that moment on, although the girl did not know why it was happening, she found it harder and harder to stay away from the small church and say no to the missionary's invitation to join the joyful people inside.

Finally, one Sunday morning the girl came inside. She opened her heart to Jesus and became a child of God. Every Sunday morning after that she came early to the church for both the Sunday School class and the service. She loved to worship and sing to Jesus and her heavenly Father. She radiated joy. The missionary was so happy with his new, little convert. On the Sunday morning she was baptized, he gave her a beautiful white dress to symbolize that the blood of Jesus Christ had washed away all her sins.

The next Sunday the missionary eagerly watched the front door as the service began, expecting the little girl to come skipping in, wearing her new white dress. He looked forward to hearing her loudly sing the songs of Zion that she had so quickly come to love. But she not did come for her Sunday School class, and the service started and ended without her. The missionary asked everyone in her Sunday School class, but no one knew why she wasn't there.

Concerned about her, the missionary hurried to the nearby village where she lived. He asked some villagers about her and was directed to her home. When he got there, he found the girl lying unconscious in the dirt just outside her front door. She was wearing her new white dress, now covered with dirt and blood.

Her father had been drinking all night, and when he saw her in the new dress, he forced her to tell him that she was going to a Christian church and had become a Christian. In a drunken rage he struck her repeatedly with his fists and kicked her until she lost consciousness. Then he threw her outdoors and left her to die in the dirt.

The missionary picked up her broken body and hurried back to the church, carrying her in his arms.

He sent for the doctor, who removed her dress and cleansed her wounds. He said there was nothing else he could do for her. Her injuries were too severe and she was dying.

Several people from the church, some of her friends from her village and the missionary stayed with her, doing what they could to comfort her in her final hours. Toward the end she regained consciousness and made an unusual request. She asked that her white dress be brought to her so she could hold it. They explained that it was torn and covered with dirt and blood, but she insisted that they bring it to her. When they did, she held it tightly against her chest.

As her eyes began to close for the last time, she whispered to those around her, "I just want Jesus to know that I was willing to bleed for Him."

Chronological Timeline of Martyrs

Jesus of Nazareth, Jerusalem, circa AD 27

Stephen, Israel, circa AD 35

Blandina & Ponticus, Roman Empire, circa AD 175

Perpetua, Felicitas, and Revocatus of Carthage, Roman Empire, circa AD 200

Nichomachus & Denisa, Roman Empire, circa 250

Peter, Roman Empire, circa AD 250

Rufina and Secunda, Roman Empire, circa AD 260

Maxima, Donatilla, & Secunda, circa AD 260

The Christian Roman Legion, AD 286

Hermenigildus, Spain: AD 586

Kiffien, Germany, AD 689

Perfectus, Spain, AD 850

Stanislus, Poland, 1079

William Tyndale, First Translator of the New Testament into English, 1536

Anne Askew, England, 1546

Lady Jane Grey, England, 1554

John Hooper & the Blind Boy, England, 1555

Margaret Wilson, Scotland, 1685

Jeanne Guyon, The 16-year-old bride who became world famous, France, 1717

Robert Thomas, Korea, 1886

Alexander Sazepa, Soviet Union, 1944

Dietrich Bonhoeffer, Germany 1945

Valentina Saveleva, Russia, circa 1965

Galia & Alexander, Soviet Union, 1966

The Bamboo Curtain, China, 1969

Heroic Christian Children, Soviet Union, 1969

Zia Nodrat, Afghanistan, circa 1970

Natalia Gorbanevskaia, Soviet Union, 1970

A Baby Martyr, China, 1970

Captain X and the 12-year-old boy, Romania, 1974

A Father & His Son, Romania, 1975

Victor Korbel, Czechoslovakia, 1975

Chiu-Chin-Hsiu and Ho-Hsiu-Tzu, China, 1977

Forever Young

Ivan Belousov, Soviet Union, 1982

Francisco, Peru, 1989

"Out of the mouth of babes . . . God has ordained strength," China, 1990

Sophie Botcharova & the Young People, Soviet Union, 1990

Yun, China, circa 1990

Mary Khoury, Lebanon, 1991

Richard Okill, South Africa, 1993

Abuk, Sudan, 1995

Linh Dao, Vietnam, circa 1995

Debbie, Egypt, circa 1997

Arsraf Masih, Pakistan, 1997

Willing to Bleed, Philippines, 1997

James Jeda, Sudan, 1998

Rachela, Nigeria, 1998

Abraham, Sudan, 1998

A Martyr's Seed, North Korea, circa 1998

Rosa, Cuba, 1998

Spartak Tagayev, Tajikistan, circa 1998

Saleema, Pakistan, 1999

Dominggus Kenjam, Indonesia, 1999

Scars of Faith, Sudan, 1999

Roy Pontoh, Indonesia, 1999

Zeba Masih, Pakistan, 1999

Cassie Bernall, United States 1999

Rachel Scott, United States, 1999

Johannes Mantahari, Indonesia, 1999

Graham, Philip, and Timothy Staines, India, 1999

Kamerino, Sudan, 2000

Maria Nenkeulah, Indonesia, 2000

Atrocities on Kasiui Island, Indonesia, 2000

Raju, India, 2000

Joshua, Nigeria, 2000

Paul Modi, Sudan, 2000

Salina, Bangladesh, circa 2000

Addil, Sudan, 2000

Safeena, Pakistan, 2001

Munira, Tajikistan, 2002

Here are some of the powerful letters VOM has received.

Greetings to you, my beloved in Jesus Christ! I greet you with Christ's words: Peace be with you. The Lord has helped me to find you. I am very happy to know that beyond our [Russian] borders there are believers too. I just happened to receive your address and am glad to be able to write to you a letter.

My name is Bogdan (which means "given by God"), and I am thirteen years old. I have a younger brother called Sascha. He is six years old. I like reading and should like to read the Bible, but have none of my own. If you have one to spare, please send it to me.

My brother cannot yet read. If you have a children's Bible with pictures in it that will reveal to him Jesus Christ, please send it to him. In my heart I shall ask the Lord's rich blessing upon you.

Lovingly yours, Bogdan

My thirteen-year-old daughter recently conducted a "Blankets of Love" drive in her small Christian school. They collected over twenty blankets and raised money to pay for all the shipping.

Thank you for your hard work and for the way you have impacted my family. You have broadened our understanding of world missions and opened our eyes to the persecuted church.

As an example of how you have impacted my daughter's thinking, I will relate this comment. We were recently walking through an expensive hotel and commented on the beautiful floor tiles. My daughter said, "Do you realize how many Bibles you could buy for the cost of that one floor tile?"

God bless you as you continue to serve our Lord.

Cindy

My name is Marina. I'm twenty-three and live in Tirana, Albania. A friend of mine gave me a book last week called Jesus Freaks. I've prayed for the persecuted Christians all over the world, but because I didn't have specific requests, I wasn't that encouraged to continue. But God is really speaking to me through this book and awakening again the desire to wrestle in prayer for my brothers and sisters.

Three years ago I started to pray regularly for Turkey every time I hear the Moslem priest's call for prayer. I admit, he is singing to Allah, but he does a perfect job to remind me that this is the time for me to ask Jesus to bring healing and salvation in Turkey. I pray for the Christians there too.

So, my brothers, I was so happy to find out through the information in the book that there are some specific ways I can help my persecuted brothers. Please send me prayer requests and any newsletters you have.

Marina

We raised money by raking leaves ($250). Our class learned about Esther and how she defended the defenseless, and now we want to help you do it too.

Each group raked about one acre of leaves!

Please walk in the light of Jesus.

God bless you,

Jesse, 4th grade

My name's Lorena and I live in Argentina. What a blessing Jesus Freaks has been to me. God has called me for serving Him in missions and that book is a great treasure that He put in my hands.

I've started praying for Pakistan and for the Christians in Kabul. I shared this with my friends and family and wrote to local newspapers for letting me talk about the obstacles and victories that my brothers and sisters in faith face every day all around the world.

I am just eighteen, but I'm standing up for Jesus Christ, and I want to serve Him because I love Him with all my heart, soul, mind, and strength.

Thank you all for opening my eyes. I'm not afraid of death now. He is my strength and refuge.

Lorena C

We recreate different types of churches in one of our Sunday School rooms for people to come, learn and be burdened for our brothers and sisters in Christ. Last year we built a church, then burned the walls and ceilings and placed it in our Sunday School room for all to come and see. We had a skit representing how the persecuted would respond to such a tragedy if they were in the church at the time.

This year we had the privilege of recreating an "underground" church. We took black plastic and camouflage netting and created a small church   within one of our Sunday School rooms. Then we built a narrow passage leading to the underground church, complete with branches and leaves from outside.

We took the congregation through the underground church to participate in a "service." We put grape juice in a plastic bag for communion, and the Pastor had only one page to the Bible hidden in his sleeve.

We have seen more and more church members become involved and support our fellow believers in Christ.

Scott and Annette C.

Hi, I am Mayone. I am eleven years old. I would like to sponsor seven dollars to your gift for Southeast Asia radio projects. If you could give a Bible or hand-cranked cassette player to a Laotian family. Thank you!

I live in Kodiak, Alaska. I go to the Kodiak Church of Christ and my friends are Hmong. My parents came from Laos. I am happy to help.

I hope to get a letter from a Laotian family when they get the Bible or hand-cranked cassette player.

Mayone K.

Could you send me the monthly newsletter and the poster? I'm only in the 6th grade, but I understand everything. I read Jesus Freaks, and now I want to learn more and help solve the problem.

I feel the Lord's call in my life to do all I can do to help my imprisoned brothers and sisters in Christ. And if I start getting the newsletter, then I can tell my friends and then all my friends will want it.

My name is Michael, and I'm eleven years old.

Oh, and if you could also send me the June issue, thanks a lot.

Your brother in Christ, Michael

P.S. My mother gave me permission to write you and thaaaannnnnk you!!! Oh, and God Bless.

Here are the proceeds from the Vacation Bible Schools at church July 17-21, and the other church July 24-28.

Our goal was to raise enough money to sponsor one hundred gospel balloons for North Korea, and one radio broadcast for Iran. For Sudan they gave   sixteen blankets, and gathered twenty-one Bibles for Nigeria. They also sent twenty-eight letters to Lo Van Hoa [a persecuted Christian in prison], to encourage him and perhaps on their own sent more.

Seventy of the kids committed to pray for a year for one Christian whose name I took from the   prisoner list. Also, the 5th and 6th grade class on their own initiative committed to pray for one country until the National Day of Prayer.

Jim D.

What Can I Do?

Perhaps after reading the stories in this book, you're asking, "What can I do? How can I help?" You may be a very young person under ten or an older young person over twenty—or somewhere in between. It doesn't matter what your age is, there IS something you can do and ways in which you can help. As someone very wise once said, "Don't count your years, make your years count!"

Following are some suggestions to help you get started.

Pray

1. The International Day of Prayer (IDOP) for the Persecuted Church occurs each November. Plan activities and programs for adults and children for IDOP. Contact The Voice of the Martyrs for information about an IDOP kit.

2. You may want to consider joining with other   families to create a VOM or LINK group to pray for the persecuted church and to work together on   projects. One example is the group "Linkers for Christ." They are a group of children ages five to twelve who pray and find creative ways to carry out VOM projects.

3. Pray for Muslims to come to Christ.

4. Pray that leaders in Muslim nations will come fact to face with Jesus' love.

5. Pray for the persecuted church traveling to and working in Muslim nations. Pray for their safety and fruit for their ministry.

6. Pray that Christians facing persecution in Muslim nations will stand firm and be a witness to their persecutors.

Raising Awareness — Possible Projects and Meetings

1. Design church bulletin inserts that share the information you are learning about the persecutionof Christians or call VOM to order the bulletins designed by VOM. Obtain your pastor's

permission to insert them in the bulletins. Ask other churches if they are interested in using your inserts.

2. Write a skit about the persecuted church and offer to perform it for other churches and youth groups. VOM will give you sample skits from readers. A VOM representative had a youth group divide up into groups and prepare skits based on the stories about persecuted Christians, such as the ones in this book.

3. Offer to be interviewed on a local radio or TV   station about what you are learning and doing about the persecution of Christians around the world.

4. Host a letter-writing session to write letters to imprisoned Christians and government officials. Consider showing a VOM video to begin the session.

a. Find the address of an official from a country where Christians are persecuted, such as an ambassador to the United States from a country where Christians are persecuted, in an up-to-date almanac or on the Internet. Write a polite letter to the official requesting that Christians in his country receive fair treatment. Do not mention politics. You may want to attach a copy of any articles you have about persecution of Christians in his country. Tell him you are praying for him.

b. Check The Voice of the Martyrs website at www.persecution.com under Ministry Opportunities for further information about writing letters on behalf of the persecuted church. For example, write to your congressmen in Washington, DC, and politely ask them to do whatever they can to help stop the killing of Christians in southern Sudan. Or write to the Sudan Embassy, 2210 Massachusetts Ave. NW, Washington, DC 20008.

c. Write letters to newspaper editors about the situation in a country where Christians are suffering for their faith. Ask them to cover the situation in their newspaper or thank them for coverage they have already done.

1. Think of creative ways for students to memorize scriptures on persecution. A group of 4,500 Romanian youth wrote out the

entire Bible in twenty-eight minutes. Each memorized a portion of Scripture and wrote it on a three-mile paper strip.

2. Provide a dinner, serving food from a country where Christians are persecuted. Give a presentation about Christians in that country. Share prayer needs of the Christians and their country, and provide information about how to get involved.

3. Decorate a bulletin board, such as the one a children's group wrote to LINK about. They update the board once a month, using a different restricted nation each month. Then they pray for the people in that nation all month.

4. A VOM Rep. provided this idea. She made fifty-three paper-chain bracelets. Each bracelet had the name of a prisoner or restricted pastor. As the congregation entered the service, she stapled a chain bracelet around each wrist and gave them an index card with information on the person named on it. She used this as a visual reminder of Hebrews 13:3 during her presentation, which ended with, "When we go home, we will probably get tired of wearing this bracelet and we can take it off. But the persecuted church can't take their chains off, so don't forget to pray for them!"

5. A youth group held weekly "fasts" to remind themselves to pray for the persecuted church. One week they gave up television, another candy, another soft drinks, etc. This group also took a church service to share about the persecuted church. They made banners, gave speeches, and made representations on various countries. For example, they dropped balloons from the church balcony to represent North Korea.

6. Teach a Sunday School class on the risks Christians face in restricted nations. VOM has a sample thirteen-week lesson plan.

7. A Sunday School teacher uses videos like Stephen's Test of Faith to develop a mission class every week. She previews the video and determines the Bible verse to teach that night. Then she asks three things to watch for in the video and quizzes the students afterwards to see if they listened. She also makes a review game, often dividing the class into teams and giving points for the correct answers. They also have a corporate prayer time, sing missions songs and spotlight the missionary the class supports. Each week they have homework that coordinates with the teaching.

8.   Role-play, answering questions about the basic beliefs of Christians. This will prepare you to defend your faith should you be called upon to do so. The person playing the interrogator could pretend they are an official in a country where Christianity is against the law. Christians have brought hostile interrogators to the Lord by showing them the love of God. One Christian woman in a communist country was questioned repeatedly by the police for her Christian activities. After she led several officers to Jesus Christ, the police made sure the same officer never questioned her twice!

9.   Hold an underground church meeting. Following are some suggestions from a VOM representative as well as others.

a.   Take time before the underground church meeting to notice the areas of faithfulness you see in the youth involved, such as witnessing at school, bringing friends to Christian meetings, playing Christian music, worshipping God, etc. Charge them with these activities.

b.   Youth leaders will bring groups of two or three to a meeting place. The house must be very dark with coverings over the windows, the electricity shut off, and everyone should sit on the floor.

c.   Certain leaders should have the responsibility to memorize Scripture to share.

d.   The music is sung with no instruments.

e.   Share testimonies of persecuted Christians.

f.   Have prearranged secret plans for the "police" to break into the meeting. They should have arrest warrants for certain youths with their names and the charges against them printed on them.

g.   Arrest the pastor or youth leader and haul them off to "prison." Keep them away during the meeting so the youth will be impacted, and use this time to tell them testimonies of faithful pastors who are in prison for such "crimes."

h.   Have a birthday cake present. Then, when the police break in, the young people have a reason to be meeting. This is what they do in many restricted countries.

i.   Show the importance of having a Bible in one's language by asking the group to get out their Bibles. No one will have brought any, so they can't. Then ask a volunteer to recite

Hebrews 13:3. If no one can, ask someone to come up and read it from your Bible, which will be in another language, for example Hmong. Of course they can't. Bring out the importance of Christians not only having a Bible, but also having one in a language they can understand.

j. Pass out "smuggled" Bible verses handwritten on cigarette-rolling paper or other small scraps of paper.

k. Share ideas of how the group can apply what they have learned by writing letters and cards to officials, keeping a prayer calendar, BASIC, bulletin inserts, etc.

l. Share the testimonies of persecuted believers. The stories of Paul Modi, Saleema, and Pastor Abraham are very effective with youth.

1. Make teaching a children/youth group about Sudan more effective by building a camp like the one pictured in a VOM newsletter, complete with a   mosquito net.

2. A VOM representative uses mannequins when she speaks to women's groups about the persecuted church. She clothes one in a dirty ragged shirt to   represent Paul Modi, a black shroud for a Muslim woman, another in Vietnamese clothing, etc. Then she walks around them as she gives testimonies of persecuted Christians.

3. Develop a VBS program or curriculum for your church using VOM/LINK resources. One church decorated five classrooms with materials from five countries served by VOM. Over a five-day span, each age group visited each country room once, learning about the country, doing crafts from the country, etc. A VBS class pretended they were Christians living in Ancient Rome at the time of persecution. They dressed in Roman costumes, hid in "catacombs," and worshipped in a "house church," while hiding from "Roman soldiers."

4. A home-school group had a meeting that focused on the persecuted church. They had three displays with prayer calendars, prisoner lists, the VOM newsletter, LINK, a sample Overcomers CD, and other materials. One part of the room was sectioned for an underground meeting and also showed video excerpts.

5. A Bible study youth group held an overnight lock-in. They had prayer sessions and VOM representatives shared. The same group collected blankets for Sudan by standing by car pool lines holding posters advertising the blanket drive. On the collection day, the drivers simply handed over their donated blankets as they drove past. A home-school group made a float advertising the "Blankets of Love" drive for a parade.

6. Organize a LINK fair using a science fair format. Let students and families exhibit reports, student-made books and displays which teach about or serve the persecuted church.

7. Encourage a representative from your church to attend a VOM Missions Conference and bring back information to share with others.

8. Show a VOM video to a group and commit to praying for the country/countries featured for a month.

9. Purchase VOM/LINK books and videos to donate to public, church and school libraries. Or start a lending library of resources about the persecuted church. Tour a Christian radio station and find out if they air VOM's segment, "The Overcomers." Ask VOM for a sample to take with you.

10. Arrange for a speaker from VOM to visit your church or group.

11. Recruit sponsors for memorizing passages of Scripture. Recite the memorized portion to the sponsor for donations to help the persecuted church.

12. A club asked people to pledge money for each letter they wrote to or on behalf of persecuted Christians in prison. They were able to raise money, encourage the persecuted, and raise awareness with the project.

13. A Sunday School class held an "I Ran for Iran" marathon as their missions project. They recruited sponsors and gave their donations to Christians in Iran.

14. Hold a Christian book and Bible drive for Christians in Nigeria. Allow people the opportunity to donate money towards shipping costs. One   mother challenged her two boys to collect a stack of Christian books as high as they were tall to give to Nigeria. They held a garage sale to pay for the shipping.

15. A children's choir raised money by putting on a musical missions program and taking up an offering.

16. A family set up a booth at a fair where they decorated faces, made animal balloons and sold candy to donate to Sudanese Christians.

17. Have a yard/craft sale, car wash, lemonade stand, etc. to raise donations for VOM/LINK projects. You may want to make crafts from a country where VOM works; for example, batik items like those made in Indonesia. Nathaniel, a ten-year-old, earned about one hundred dollars for a VOM project at a lemonade stand he and his brothers set up at a community yard sale.

18. John, age seven, raised money for Sudanese Christians by designing and distributing a flyer to family and friends that told about the needs of   persecuted Christians.

19. Ask for donations or sell tickets for a presentation or event you will put on. Ideas would be a play,   puppet show, musical performance, fair booth, a tournament of a game from a restricted nation, a fashion show of native dress, etc.

20. Skip a meal a day or dessert, using the money saved to give towards specific needs or countries. Spend the skipped mealtime in prayer for the people or project to which you will contribute.

21. Collect spare change in a jar for a year.

22. One family set aside a month to collect as many blankets as they could. The children went door to door, announced their project in church and set up a table to collect them.

23. To raise money for Sudanese Christians, one family held a "Cans for Sudan" drive.

24. One youth group used proceeds from their soft drink machine to help purchase Bibles for China.

25. Some young people have sold produce from a garden or eggs from their chickens to provide money to VOM projects.

Here are some examples of young people who also asked,
"What can I do?" They will inspire you!

"Seven years ago . . . the Lord . . . placed a desire to help the many children of India," said Sheena C. "Since then I have seen God working to make sure I get to India."

In 2001, Sheena got a summer job with the forest service to earn money to go to India. Members of her church also added to her trip fund. God led Sheena to people who helped her make arrangements to work in India caring for orphaned Indian girls and teaching them English.

"There is a verse I want to share that God has given me," she said. "It says, 'Whom shall I send and who will go for us? Then I said, Here am I. Send me.'"

What does her family think about her traveling to a country so far away?

"I've told Sheena many times," said her mother, "it's better to die walking in the will of God than to live walking out of it. I believe she is in God's hands."

Ten-year-old Philippe and eight-year-old Joel attend a Christian school. They learned about James Ladula, a young persecuted Christian who lives in Sudan, from their father, who works for The Voice of the Martyrs. During a visit to their grandfather's home, Philippe and Joel learned to enjoy can hunting — collecting aluminum cans for recycling. After they returned home, they decided they wanted to use can money to help "Jimmy," as they called James.

Word about their project spread around their school and neighborhood, and others joined them in can collecting. In their first trip to the recycling   center to sell the aluminum cans that were collected, they got $14 for Jimmy. Special can containers were set up at VOM headquarters to encourage others to collect "Cans for Kids of Courage."

As one employee said, "Sacks of cans are multiplying just like the loaves and fishes another small boy gave to Jesus long ago."

Do you know places where you could go can hunting or someplace you could set up special "Cans for Kids of Courage" containers?

For stories about "Kids of Courage," see The Voice of Martyrs web site for young people at: http://www.linkingup.com.

Thirteen-year-old David G. helps support a   persecuted pastor with money earned by tractoring, cleaning horse stalls, painting fences and working as a field hand. He has also shared about VOM's Pastor Support Program (PSP) at his church.

Six-year-old Garrett, four-year-old Madison, and two-year-old Tanner learned about their PSP pastor from their grandmother Myrtle. Their grandmother sends $25.00 a month to VOM for the pastor to feed and clothe his family of four. She gave the kids photos of the pastor, which they keep by their bed.

Every night, Garrett, Madison and Tanner ask God to help their pastor meet his needs, like "wood, a roof, books about Jesus and a microphone [to tell more people about Jesus]," said Garrett.

"And macaroni!" added Madison.

Index

CREATION

Adam and Eve driven from Garden Cain slays Abel

Noah Builds Ark

The Flood

Tower of Babel built

Jericho founded, world's first walled town

Society in Japan based on hunting, fishing and gathering

Japanese pottery with geometric motifs. Greek farmers clear forests for farming

3,500 First great Sumerian civilizations emerge along Nile-Egypt and Mesopotamia

4,236- first date in Egyptian calendar

First use of plow by farmers in Britain

Llamas and alpacas domesticated in Peru; widespread cultivation of maize, potatoes and corn in North, Central and South America.

Farming begins in China

3,500 Invention of the wheel in Mesopotamia

3,372 first date in Maya calendar

3,200 Earliest surviving evidence of writing in Temple of Urk in Mesopotamia

c. 2,600 Building of Stonehenge, Britain

2,572-2,464 Great Pyramids of Cheops, Giza completed, one of the Seven Wonders of the World

Abraham chosen by God

God destroys Sodom and Gomorrah

---

c. 2000 Rise of Old Babylon

1,760 Hammurabi's Code-greatest warrior-ruler of Babylon created code written in cuneiform, first exercise in history to develop a civilized way of life. The Codes addressed criminal civil matters, from murder to family disputes Isaac born to Abraham and Sarai

c. 1,600 Minoans erect palace at Knossos, in Crete.

Rise of Dong-Son culture in Vietnam, spreads across Southeast Asia

Egyptians develop mathematics

1,678 Joseph, favorite son of Jacob, sold by his brothers to be a slave

1,666 Joseph 2nd in command in Egypt

1,657 Children of Jacob (who is now called Israel) follow Joseph to live in Egypt

1,595 Hittites from Anatolia penetrate northern borders of the Babylonian empire

1,523-1,027 Bronze and jade objects are created during the Shang dynasty in China

c. 900 Olmec civilization in Mexico. Villages along Mexican Gulf Coast have irrigation system

Earliest surviving Native American town in North America - Mississippi

Development of the Hindu culture of Ganges valley

1,600-717 The Hittites smelt and forge iron, technique increased carbon content of iron

1,391-1,353 Reign of Pharaoh Amenhotep II Egypt's Golden Age

1,304-1,237 Pharaoh Ramese II's kingdom-Nubia to the Nile Delta.

Moses found in the bulrushes by Pharaoh's daughter

1,250-1,210 Moses leads Jewish people in flight from Egypt to Palestine

Moses gives the Ten Commandments to the Jews

The Ark of the Covenant is constructed

Moses dies and the Israelites cross into the Promised Land

c. 1,400 Battle of Jericho; walls of the city collapse

Caste system-rigid hierarchical structure in Indian society

Siege of Troy

Rule of Judges among the Israelites

Gideon leads small army into victory over the Midianites.

Samson betrayed by Delilah

1100 Phoenicians develop script, which will become the basis of all European scripts.

Time of the Jewish prophets

Samuel anoints Saul to be King of Israel

Samuel anoints David to be King

1,003 David, King of Israel, establishes capital at Jerusalem

971 David dies; his son Solomon succeeds him as king

960 Solomon builds Temple on Mount Morriah

Great period of Tyre in Phoenicia

Culture of Villanova flourishes in Italy

After Solomon, Jeroboam leads revolt against Rheoboam in kingdom of Judea

Damascus is center of power and trade

c. 900 Foundation of Sparta, Greece-city of military training and strength

Elijah taken up in a whirlwind in a chariot of fire

C.850 Homer composes The Illiad and The Odyssey

814 Phoenicians found City of Carthage

Sardinia known for distinctive architecture and bronze sculptures

Isaiah, the prophet

Micah

Beginning of Etruscan period in Italy

Chariots introduced into Italy by Etruscans

776 first Olympic games held in Greece

753 Legendary foundation of Rome on banks of Tiber, by Romulus, first of seven kings

715 King Numa Pompilius, of Rome, establishes 12-month calendar.

700 first coins used in Lydia, Turkey

650 Greek historian Herodotus noted Phoenicians circumnavigate Africa

Lifetime of Jeremiah, Ezekiel, Daniel, Zechariah

City of Jerusalem falls to Babylonians; Solomon's Temple destroyed

551 Confucious born

550 Siddhartha Gautama Buddah, founder of Buddism, born

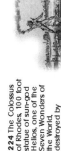

First code of law issued in China

509 Roman Republic founded; Etruscans driven from city

Roman Monarchy replaced by two consuls elected by popular assemblies

278 First Roman treaty with Carthage

437 Completion of the Parthenon, Greece

Life of Nehemiah

399 Trial and execution of Socrates

387 Plato founded academy in Athens

336-323 Alexander the Great succeeded King Philip II of Macedonia. Alexander conquered Asia Minor, Armenia, Palestine, Egypt and Persia; his empire reached from Indus Valley to eastern sections of Mediterranean and northern portions of Africa

312 Construction of Appian Way-route from Rome to Brindisi, approx. 350 miles

297-280 425 foot-tall lighthouse of port in Alexandria is built; One of the Seven Wonders of the World

275 The mathematician Euclid sets principles of geometry in Elements

284 Ptolemy founded Museum in Alexandria dedicated to Muses

Start of translation of Hebrew holy scriptures into Greek

224 The Colossus of Rhodes, 100 foot statue of sun-god Helios, one of the Seven Wonders of the World, destroyed by earthquake

221 The Great Wall of China built, 2,600-mile-long wall

215 Roman army defeats Hannibal at battle of Zama

Rome now a major Mediterranean power

551 Confucianism becomes state religion in China

206 Zhang Qian established "Silk Roads," links central Asia to the Mediterranean

Roman roads link Italy with Spain, also coast roads from Alps to the Rhone

Roman trading posts extend from southwest coast of India to southern edge of Sahara Desert

119 3/4 Goods carried on "Silk Road" from China to Europe

70-63 Rule of Pompey over Roman Empire

64 Pompey annexes Judea as a Roman province

55 Caesar invades Britain

52 Caesar begins his Roman conquest of Gaul

50 Cleopatra becomes Queen of Egypt

Rome's civil war ends in defeat of Mark Anthony & Cleopatra, at Actium, Greece

Pompey, sole consul, commands Caesar to disband army

Caesar crosses Rubicon river, marches into Italy

Pompey is murdered in Egypt

Julius Caesar is the supreme ruler of Rome

44 March 15th, Julius Caesar assassinated in Rome, an event that marks the beginning of the decline of the Roman Empire

Roman Senate appoints Herod the Great as King of Judea

6-4 Birth of Jesus Christ in Bethlehem

Death of Herod the Great

Roman Empire divided by three sons associated with the Murder of the Innocents

Pontius Pilate serves as Procurator of Judea

John the Baptist denounces Herod Antipas for incestuous marriage to Herodias

27 April 30, Crucifixion of Jesus Christ in Palestine at Golgatha

29 Descent of the Holy Spirit on Pentecost

35 Stephen, first Christian martyr

36-68 Buddhism flourishes in Asia

37 On Road to Damascus, Syria Saul of Tarsus converted to Christianity by vision of Jesus Christ; now named Paul, he begins missionary work

64 Rome; Emperor Nero, Great Fire; persecution of Christians

66 First Jewish revolt against Rome. Jesus brother, James, and Paul martyred

First apostle martyred-James

The apostle Peter crucified

54 The apostle Philip dies

63 James (the Less) dies

64 Barnabas, a missionary who traveled with Paul, dies

64 The apostle Mark dies

Jews rise up against Romans in Judea

68-70 Dead Sea Scrolls hidden in caves

69 The apostle Paul dies

69 The apostle Peter dies

70 The apostle Matthew dies

70 The apostle Thomas dies

70 The apostle Andrew dies

70 AD September 7, under siege by Vespasian's son, Titus, Jerusalem falls to Romans, and the Temple is destroyed

70 The apostle Luke dies

90s Early church structure established, bishops, presbyters, and deacons

95 John the Apostle, while on the Isle of Patmos, receives his Revelation of Jesus Christ

c.100 AD Buddhism reaches China from Asia and India

105 Paper invented

100-c.165 Justin Martyr describes the liturgical worship of the Church, centered in the Eucharist

c.130-c.200 Irenaeus

c.150-c.212 Tertullian

220 Iron-smelting develops in East Africa

250 Persecution of Christians under Decius

303 Persecution of Christians under Diocletian

313 Constantine I grants tolerance to the Christians in the Roman Empire

325 Council of Nicaea settles heretical challenge to the Christian faith

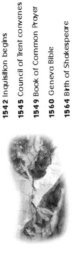

331-420 Jerome

354-430 Augustine of Hippo

361 Birth of Attila the Hun

387 Augustine converted to Christianity

397 North African Council, Carthage, determines canon; Jerome translates Vulgate

440 Pope Leo I proclaims supremacy of papacy in governing Christianity

450 Chief Hawai-Loa discovers Hawaiian Islands

450 Bodhidharma founds Zen Buddhism, India; takes to China

451 Council of Chalcedon affirms apostolic doctrine of two natures in Christ, divine and human

476 Fall of Rome to Goths

525 Dionysius Exiguus sets birth of Jesus and Christian calendar at Dec. 23, AD1

537 King Arthur killed at Camelot

542-594 Plague cuts population of Europe in half

622 Birth of Islamic religion

640 Library of Alexandria with 30,000 manuscripts completely destroyed

700 Beowulf composed between 700-750

732 Battle of Poitiers- victory from Franks kept Islam out of Christian Europe

800 Charlemagne crowned Holy Roman emperor

831 Dublin founded

982 Greenland discovered by, Eric the Red

988 Vladimir converts, brings Christianity to Kiev and Russia

1000 Viking Leif Erickson discovers North America

1000 Gunpowder discovered in China

1054 East-West church schism

1085 King Alfonso VI conquers Toledo, the old Visigothic capital, and discovers the works of Aristotle, Plato, and Muhammed abu-Muhammed al-Ghazali

1096 First Christian crusade to the Holy Land

1100s Norman, then Gothic, cathedrals are built

1118 The fall of Zaragoza to Christian forces

1170 Murder of Thomas Becket, Archbishop of Canterbury

1182 Magnetic compass discovered

1204 Sack of Constantinople by Rome adds to the estrangement between East and West

1207 Genghis Khan overruns Asia

1225-1274 Thomas Aquinas

1270 eighth and last Christian crusade

1298 Marco Polo writes The Travels of Marco Polo

1325 Aztecs build their capital, Tenochtitlan,

1337-1453 Hundred Years War between France and England

1342-1400 Chaucer, English author, The Canterbury Tales

1347 Black Plague kills 75 million - halts economic growth in Europe for 200 years

1350-1527 Approximate dates of the Renaissance

1362-1415 Jan Huss, must important Czech religious reformer

1368 China, Ming Dynasty

1330-c. – 1384 John Wycliffe translates the Bible into English

1378-1417 Great Schism brings an end to papal domination

1380-1471 Thomas A Kempis, author of The Imitation of Christ, first pub.1427

1386-1466 Donatello, great Florentine sculptor

1431 Joan of Arc burned at the stake in France

1452-1519 Leonardo da Vinci sculptor, architect, engineer, and scientist

1453 Fall of Constantinople to the Turks

1450 Johann Gutenberg invents the printing press

1455 Gutenberg prints the first Bible

1469-1527 Niccolo Machiavelli, Italian Philosopher, author of The Prince

1473-1543 Nicolaus Copernicus, Polish Astronomer, founder of modern astronomy

1475-1564 Michelangelo, sculptor and painter in Florence; The Pieta, Moses, David and the Sistine Chapel

1488 The Portuguese rounded the cape of Africa

1492 Columbus discovers America - 1495 proves the world is round

1497 The Florentine John Cabot discovered the North American continent

1483-1546 Martin Luther

1490-1536 William Tyndale

1509-1564 John Calvin

1489-1556 Thomas Cranmer

1491-1556 Ignatius Loyola

1514-1572 John Knox

1500s Spanish conquer Aztec, Inca civilizations in the New World

1502 Shidism becomes state religion in Persia

1516-1587 John Foxe, author of The Foxe's Book of Martyrs, pub. 1563

1517 Martin Luther posts his 95 theses, Protestant Reformation begins

1525 William Tyndale translates the New Testament from Greek into English

1533-1584 Ivan the Terrible rules Russia

1534 Society of Jesus (Jesuits) founded

1536 Tyndale strangled and burned

1536 King Henry VIII breaks with the Church of Rome and founds The Church of England

1542 Inquisition begins

1545 Council of Trent convenes

1549 Book of Common Prayer

1560 Geneva Bible

1564 Birth of Shakespeare

1572 Saint Bartholomew Day Massacre of 50,000 Protestants in France

1600s English, French, Dutch colonize North America, East and West Indies

South Africa: kill or enslave and evangelize native peoples

1607 Authorised King James Version of the Bible

1607 Jamestown, first English settlement in North America

1623-1662 Blaise Pascal

1616-1683 John Owen

1626-1688 John Bunyan

1614-1691 Brother Lawrence, author of The Practice of the Presence of God, pub. in parts 1691, 1741

1620 Pilgrims, aboard the Mayflower, land at Plymouth Rock

1628-1688 John Bunyan, author of The Pilgrim's Progress, first pub. 1668

1633 Galileo convicted of heresy for writing Dialogue on Great World Systems

1640-1660 English Civil War and Protectorate

1648 Westminster Confession

1648-1717 Madame Jeanne Guyon, author of Experiencing Union with God Through Inner Prayer and the Way and Results of Union with God, pub. 1685

1662 -1714 Mathew Henry

1667 John Milton publishes Paradise Lost

1703-1758 Jonathan Edwards

1714-1770 George Whitfield

1720-1750 Great Awakening in America

1703-1790 John Wesley

1763 Seven Year War in Europe

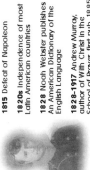

1760 The Industrial Revolution begins in England

1781 American Revolution

1799 French Revolution

1792-1875 Charles Finney

1795-1835 Second Great Awakening in America

1703-1758 Johnathan Edwards

1703-1791 John Wesley

1707-1788 Charles Wesley

1714-1770 George Whitefield

1800s Missionary organizations translate Bible into many languages

1815 Defeat of Napoleon

1820s Independence of most Latin American countries

1828 Noah Webster publishes An American Dictionary of the English Language

1828-1917 Andrew Murray, author of With Christ in the School of Prayer, first pub. 1885

1759-1833 William Wilberforce

1761-1834 William Carey

1780-1845 Elizabeth Fry

1792-1875 Charles Finney

1805-1898 George Muller

1813-1873 David Livingstone

1834-1892 C.H. Spurgeon

1837-1899 D.L. Moody

1829-1912 General Wm. Booth, founder of the Salvation Army

1856-1928 R.A. Torrey

1832-1911 Hannah Whitall Smith, author of The Christian's Secret to a Happy Life, first pub. 1875

1892 Charles H. Spurgeon, author of Morning By Morning

1837-1897 Dwight Lyman Moody

1844 Samuel Frank Morse invents the telegraph

1845 Irish Potato famine - nearly 1 million people die

1848 Karl Marx publishes Das Capital

1857-1858 Third Great Awakening in America Prayer Meeting Revival

1859 Darwin publishes The Origin of Species

1851-1897 Henry Drummond, author of The Greatest Thing in the World, first pub. 1884

1857-1946 Charles Sheldon, author of In His Steps, first pub. 1896

1861-1864 American Civil War

1867-1934 Madame Marie Curie, discovers radium, wins Nobel Prize in 1903 for physics and in 1911 for chemistry

1867 Alexander Graham Bell invents the telephone

1881-1955 Sir Alexander Fleming discovers penicillin in 1929

1886-1952 A.W. Pink

1898-1900 Boxer Rebellion in China

1898-1963 C.S. Lewis

1901 American Standard Version of the Bible first pub.

1906-1909 Azusa Street Revival California

1912-1984 Francis A. Schaeffer

1914-1918 World War I

1894 Jonas Salk born, US bacteriologist, develops the Salk Vaccine to inoculate against polio

1917 Bolshevik Revolution in Russia

1923 J. Gresham Machen, fundamentalist leader, writes Christianity and Liberalism

1926 Scope Trial pits literal reading vs. modern understanding of the Bible

---

1929 American Stock Market crashes, starts 12-year long Great Depression

1939-1945 World War II

1947 Dead Sea Scrolls found

1948 State of Israel established

1949 Communist revolution in China; Christianity suppressed

1952 Revised Standard Version of the Bible published

1959 Chinese invade Tibet

1960s Civil Rights movement US

1960s Post colonial independence of most African and Asian countries

1966 Neil Armstrong walks on the moon

1989 Berlin Wall comes down - opens Eastern Germany to Christianity

1989 New Revised Standard Version of the Bible first pub. Dead Sea Scrolls made widely available

1990s Internet technology globalizes communication; economy globalizes

1906-1945 Dietrich Bonhoeffer

1991 Communist Government in Russia crumbles; Christianity regains its liberty

1998 Another space travel for John Glenn, age 77, worlds oldest astronaut

2001 September 11th Terrorist Attack on U.S.